Entrepreneurship and how to establish your own business

4th edition

Johan Strydom (Editor)
Cecile Nieuwenhuizen (Consulting Editor)

JUTA

Entrepreneurship and how to establish your own business

First published 1996
Second edition 2001
Third edition 2007
Fourth edition 2012

Juta and Company Ltd
First floor
Sunclare Building
21 Dreyer street
Claremont
7708
PO Box 14373, Lansdowne, 7779, Cape Town, South Africa

ISBN 978-0-70218-920-3

Typeset in 10/12 Corporate A
Project Manager: Debbie Henry
Editor: Helen Hacksley
Proofreader: Willemien Jansen
Indexer: Sanet le Roux
Typesetter: ANdtp Services
Cover designer: Eugene Badenhorst

Printed in South Africa by Impressum Print Solutions

Contents

Preface

It is generally accepted that additional support is needed to start a business in the dynamic environment in which entrepreneurs operate. This updated 4th edition of *Entrepreneurship and how to establish your own business* aims to guide aspiring entrepreneurs who have the will and desire to start and manage their own business and want to do this successfully. It is often said that entrepreneurship comes naturally and that the entrepreneur knows instinctively how to start a business. However, entrepreneurs need all the support that they can get and it is always beneficial to learn from other successful entrepreneurs how to avoid making unnecessary mistakes.

This book reflects the combined experience of the authors in the fields of small-business management and entrepreneurship. This experience has been gained through interviews, consultation and primary research done in their academic fields of specialisation.

The result of this experience is a book which is a practical guide to analyse yourself and your abilities critically, to evaluate business ideas with an open mind and to plan your business proactively. We aim to communicate how to:

- be positive and use even your seemingly most insignificant talents, skills and knowledge, whilst acknowledging your weak points;
- be creative yet practical in your search for business ideas and to believe in whatever business venture you attempt;
- research your business idea and ensure that it will be profitable; and
- plan your business carefully and learn how to handle important issues such as financing the start-up and marketing the business.

The willingness to learn is the first step in realising your dream to start your own business. If you have the desire to be successful, it is possible to achieve success. We hope this book will make you enthusiastic about learning more and doing better in your business venture. Good luck!

Johan Strydom
Pretoria
August 2011

About the authors

Dr Alex Antonites is a Senior Lecturer in the Department of Business Management and Chair for Entrepreneurship at the University of Pretoria. He specialises in the field of entrepreneurship and small business development with a specific focus on the pre-entrepreneurial phase concerning creativity, innovation and opportunity finding. Alex has published in local and international journals, with a specific focus on entrepreneurship education, training and development.

Andreas de Beer is a Senior Lecturer in the Department of Business Management at the University of South Africa (Unisa).

Prof Michael Cant is Head of the Marketing and Retail Department at the University of South Africa (Unisa).

Prof Hannelize Jacobs is an Associate Professor in Management and Head of the Department of Management at Monash South Africa (a campus of Monash University, Australia). She holds a DCom Strategic Management degree and focuses her research on strategically managing and leading entrepreneurship and innovation in organisations. Over the years she has been involved in numerous strategic innovation experiments herself. She believes that what is needed today is a new competency set for socio-cognitive learning and innovation in organisations.

Prof Cecile Nieuwenhuizen was the Head of the Department of Business Management at the University of South Africa (Unisa). She is currently the Head of the Department of Business Management at the University of Johannesburg (UJ). She has written several books and articles in journals on entrepreneurship and business management. She is also involved as director in various family businesses. Cecile is the co-ordinating editor of Juta's Entrepreneurship Series.

Prof Johan Wilhelm Strydom was appointed as Professor in Business Management in the School of Management Sciences at the University of South Africa (Unisa) in 1993. He has authored/co-authored numerous textbooks and accredited articles. His research interests are in the fields of small business, strategic marketing and international marketing.

CHAPTER ONE

Entrepreneurship and small, medium and micro enterprises (SMMEs) in perspective

Cecile Nieuwenhuisen

Learning outcomes

After you have studied this chapter, you should be able to:

- define the term 'entrepreneur'
- indicate the similarities and differences between entrepreneurship, a small business enterprise and small business management
- know which key factors contribute to successful entrepreneurship
- give a critical evaluation of
  - personal skills, expertise and aptitude
  - personal characteristics
  - functional management skills.

1.1 Introduction

Economic development can be directly attributed to the level of entrepreneurial activity in a country. In high-growth, globally competitive economies the ability to nurture this entrepreneurial activity and grow businesses, create wealth and sustain competitive advantage is imperative. This is because there is a direct correlation between job creation and the level of entrepreneurial activity in an economy, as well as a positive, statistically significant association between national economic growth and entrepreneurship. According to Kao (1993) entrepreneurial businesses ensure growth in the economy by doing something new and/or innovative to create wealth for the entrepreneur and to add value to society.

Definition

The **entrepreneur** is 'a person who undertakes a wealth-creating and value-adding process, through developing ideas, assembling resources and making things happen' (Kao, Kao & Kao, 2002:42).

There are various definitions of an entrepreneur but one significant point is that entrepreneurs are people with the ability to identify an opportunity and create and grow a business. They are able to combine their creative ideas with the necessary skills, resources and people to form a successful business.

Example

An entrepreneur can therefore be described as someone who:

- starts their own business
- manages their own business
- identifies new products or opportunities
- is creative and/or innovative
- organises and controls resources (such as capital, labour, materials) to ensure a profit
- has the ability and insight to market, produce and finance a service or product
- has financial means or who can obtain financing so as to realise the enterprise
- is willing to take calculated risks.

This summary of general capabilities clearly indicates the role of an entrepreneur in establishing and running a business.

It is important to keep in mind that not everyone who starts a new business is, in reality, an entrepreneur. Some might be *enterprising* but true entrepreneurs habitually *create and innovate* to build and grow something of recognised value. Not all small, medium and micro enterprises (SMMEs) achieve anything new or different, nor do they all grow and become successful. Thus, although small businesses contribute to wealth creation and add value to the economy, not all SMMEs are necessarily *entrepreneurial*.

SMMEs, not necessarily entrepreneurial businesses, form 97% of all businesses in South Africa. Of these, 46% are micro businesses, 36% very small businesses, 11% small businesses, 4 % medium businesses and 3% large businesses. SMMEs generate up to 34% of the Gross Domestic Product (GDP) and contribute 43% of the total value of salaries and wages paid in South Africa and employ 55% of all the formal private-sector employees (dti, 2008: 28). In contrast, in the US, Japan and Germany, small businesses contribute more than 50% to the GDP in each country.

Definition

Gross Domestic Product (GDP) is the total production of a country. The total number of services and products supplied and produced within the borders of a country in one year are measured in financial terms by the GDP. The growth rate of GDP is an indication of how successful a country is in providing jobs and income to its citizens.

1.2 The relationship between entrepreneurship and small business management

Most businesses begin as small or micro enterprises and are usually managed by one person. The aim of that person is to grow the business. This can happen continuously as long as the entrepreneur retains his or her entrepreneurial mindset (ie continues to innovate and create). However, if the entrepreneur becomes comfortable and satisfied with the level of growth within the enterprise, he or she stops being an entrepreneur and becomes a small business manager, who is risk-, change- and innovation-averse. Schumpeter (1934) observes that most firms settle for this non-entrepreneurial stability, and Gray (2002) confirms this low intention to grow in most small businesses.

Example

Examples of a small business manager who is not an entrepreneur are:

- a person who manages an existing business or franchise without ensuring growth
- a person who inherits a business and runs it in the same way as his or her predecessor
- a person who is appointed by the owner of a small business as the manager.

There is a certain danger at this point in the business's development; even though the entrepreneur may have good ideas and be competent, he or she may not have the necessary skills to manage a small business. This lack of managerial skills could cause the business to fail. To be successful, the small business manager must be able to:

- plan, organise, lead and control the various business functions
- organise the efficient operation of tasks
- ensure interpersonal and inter-group competence
- facilitate formal communication during scheduled meetings
- compile and implement necessary policies and procedures for the business.

1.3   Types of entrepreneurial businesses

Entrepreneurial businesses can be classified as either informal, micro, very small, small, medium or large. Each type of business has very specific characteristics with specific needs and features. We will discuss some of these in the following section.

The National Small Business Amendment Act (No. 26 of 2003) has set out criteria defining business size in each sector of industry (see Table 1.1 on p. 4).

1.3.1   The formal small business

The small and micro business sector

In the National Small Business Amendment Act of South Africa (No. 26 of 2003) a micro business is defined as a business with five or fewer employees and a turnover of up to R100 000. A very small business employs between one and ten employees, and a small business between 11 and 50 employees. The upper limit for turnover in a small business varies between R3 million in the Agricultural sector to R13 million in the Manufacturing and Catering, Accommodation and other Trade sectors, with a maximum of R32 million in the Wholesale Trade sector. The upper limits for employment and turnover in the various sectors are indicated in Table 1.1.

Table 1.1: Definition of a small business according to industrial sector, employment and turnover

Sector or sub-sector in accordance with the Standard Industrial Classification	The total full-time equivalent of paid employees	Total turnover
Agriculture	50	R3m
Mining and Quarrying	50	R10m
Manufacturing	50	R13m
Electricity, Gas and Water	50	R13m
Construction	50	R6m
Retail and Motor Trade and Repair Services	50	R19m
Wholesale Trade, Commercial Agents and Allied Services	50	R32m
Catering, Accommodation and other trade	50	R13m
Transport, Storage and Communications	50	R13m
Finance and Business Services	50	R13m
Community, Social and Personal Services	50	R6m

Adapted from *National Small Business Amendment Act*, (No 26 of 2003)

Successful entrepreneurs provide inspiration and act as role models. We have all heard of exceptional entrepreneurs such as Bill Gates and Mark Shuttleworth, but there are many lesser known people with whom we can more easily associate. Examples can be found in all sectors of the economy, and vary from micro businesses in basic products and services to sophisticated IT companies and highly professional practices, with all types of creative, entrepreneurial businesses in between. Here are some examples in the small business category:

Example

Passion on a Plate is an entrepreneurial concern in the Catering, Accommodation and Other Trade sector. Two students, Eduan Naude and Stan Louw, started a catering company with R150 as an entrepreneurship assignment for a university programme in 2003. After less than two years, they had achieved a turnover of R70 000 per month. Their business now includes catering for weddings and other functions, team building and cooking classes. Recently, they also opened a restaurant and guest house.

Ezabantu Fishing is another inspirational micro enterprise that grew to become a successful small business. It began because the owner, Bulelwa Qupe, could not find enough fish for her fish-and-chips shop. She acquired a fishing quota, began fishing and soon had too much fish for her own needs. This prompted her to establish her own export company, Buntu Marketing and Exporting, which exports white hake to Spain and abalone to Asia.

⮥

Decorex, South Africa's international interior decorating showcase, was started with a few hundred rand by Nicola Hadfield ten years ago. She first approached Decorex in London to start a similar show in South Africa, but they regarded South Africa as too Third World for a decorating show of the calibre of Decorex. She decided to proceed on her own and the show has become a huge success. After eight successful years in operation, Nicola sold the show to a Dutch company so that she can pursue new business opportunities. She is a typical 'habitual' entrepreneur.

Andre and Gary Shearer established **Cape Classics Inc.** in 1992. It began as a small wine export company in Cape Town and has developed into two separate award-winning companies: Cape Classics Export based in Cape Town and Cape Classics Inc. based in New York. They achieved this success in only ten years.

Andre Shearer set up Cape Classics Inc. in New York in 1992. His company has since been honoured in the annual American Wine Awards as the best wine importer to the USA. This award is given by the *Food and Wine Magazine*—a very influential American publications, which targets the affluent American customer. Andre's award is the first to a South African specialist import company.

Start-up capital for Cape Classics was provided by the Small Business Development Corporation (SBDC) (now Business Partners). In 1996 and 1997 Cape Classics received the President's Award for export. The Shearer brothers attribute their success to perseverance, knowledge of basic business principles, the quality of their products and the excellent service they provide.

1.4   Corporate entrepreneurship/intrapreneurship

Corporate entrepreneurship (or intrapreneurship) is also a form of entrepreneurship. This is when a new business is created within an existing business but with products or services different from the original business. The corporate entrepreneur identifies a specific business opportunity and establishes a new business within an existing business.

Definition

Corporate entrepreneurship (intrapreneurship) is the creation of a business or businesses within an existing large business, by using new ideas and opportunities. The new and relatively small autonomous business unit produces a product or service using the resources of an existing business.

Corporate entrepreneurship makes it possible for large businesses to adapt to changes in the market entrepreneurially, to experiment in the market, to diversify from the core business, to establish new distribution channels and to make profits from new businesses.

> ### *Example*
>
> An example of corporate entrepreneurship is First National Bank (FNB), which used to be a conventional bank only. Subsequently FNB ventured into new businesses such as Outsurance and Discovery Health. Outsurance is a short-term insurance company and a diversification of FNB's core business. When Outsurance was established it was different in that it offered direct, short-term insurance to individuals without the traditional intermediary insurance brokers. Outsurance has grown from a small corporate entrepreneurial business to a large insurance business.

1.4.1   Franchisors and franchisees

> ### *Definition*
>
> **Franchising** is an arrangement whereby one person or business (the franchisor) grants an independent party (the franchisee) the right to sell the business's products or services according to guidelines set down by the franchisor. The franchisor retains control over the conduct of the business and offers the franchisee a comprehensive business package. Examples of franchises are Steers Takeaways and Blockbusters Video shops.

The franchisor is an entrepreneur, whereas the franchisee should rather be seen as a corporate entrepreneur (or intrapreneur) possibly initiating innovative ideas within the franchise system.

Franchisees do not have the freedom to experiment, operate and market their business based on their own vision of how things should be done but must adhere to the plans of the franchisor. However, a recent study proved that franchisees do show an entrepreneurial orientation in certain situations, such as multiple-outlet franchisees (Maritz, 2005). Franchisors in many sectors have recognised the benefit of multiple-unit franchisees (Johnson, 2004), and this is seen as an entrepreneurial continuation of the franchise trend.

Franchisors usually fall into the medium to large business category, as the more successful franchisors manage a large number of franchises apart from the overall management of the franchise group. In South Africa alone there are 391 franchise systems, of which 90.5% originated and were developed in South Africa. International franchise systems operating within South Africa number 37. The franchise systems combined are responsible for 22 825 outlets, employing 284 447 people, according to the 2004 census by the Franchise Advice and Information Network (FRAIN). The contribution of the franchise industry to GDP is 11% (FRAIN Franchise Census, 2004).

Franchisees can fall anywhere between the small to medium categories.

> ### *Example*
>
> Ten years ago, Kobus Oosthuizen started a bakery franchise called Butterfield Bakery. Kobus's franchise operation now has more than 120 franchisees. What is different about Butterfield Bakery outlets is that they have a defined market and are situated close to their target markets (mines and other areas inadequately serviced by traditional or in-house bakeries). The combined turnover of these franchises is more than R300 million per annum.
>
> More familiar to the public is Nando's. This franchise was started in the south of Johannesburg 18 years ago by Robert Brozin and Fernando Duarte as a fast-food shop selling spicy, grilled chicken meals. In 2001 there were 343 Nando's worldwide. Of these, 184 are within South Africa, 70 are owned by Nando's, and 159 are international, situated mainly in Britain, Australia and the Middle East.

1.5   Key success factors of entrepreneurs

Entrepreneurs possess particular characteristics that set them apart. This does not mean that all entrepreneurs have the same characteristics or combination of characteristics. Some entrepreneurs are successful because they are prepared to take chances, while others achieve their goals largely as a result of their innovative skills and flair for management. Each entrepreneur has a unique combination of factors at his/her disposal for achieving success. In fact, research has shown that there is no typical entrepreneur because few, if any, entrepreneurs possess all of the characteristics or skills we will discuss.

The following figure summarises the key success factors that usually contribute to successful entrepreneurship.

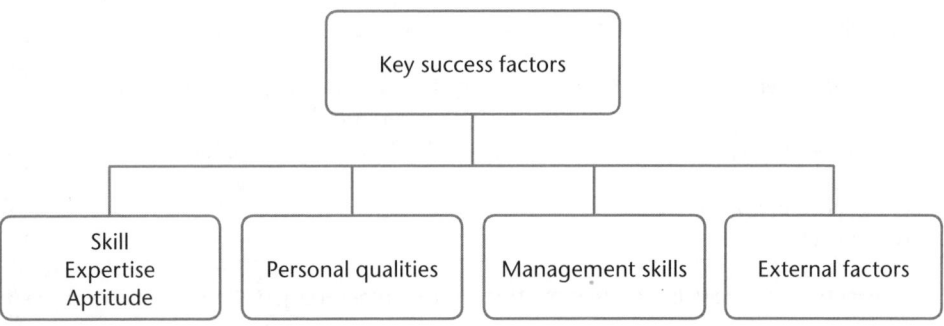

Figure 1.1: Key success factors

As an entrepreneur, it is important for you to analyse your personal strengths and weaknesses. Strengths can then be positively applied and weaknesses can be addressed by one or more of the following:

*   personal development
*   attending courses
*   appointing staff and/or experts to compensate where needed.

1.5.1 The skills, expertise and aptitudes of an entrepreneur

Successful entrepreneurs have particular skills, expertise and aptitudes that can be applied profitably in any business. It is best to start or run a business with something you feel comfortable and know a lot about (expertise) and/or in which you are skilled. The match between you, as the person starting the business, and the type of business is therefore most important.

Definition

Skills usually refer to manual work and can be learned. You can learn to become, for example, an electrician, a hairdresser or cabinet-maker.

Expertise is based on knowledge you acquire. Expertise and knowledge are obtained by studying and/or experience. There are experts in fields such as taxation, computer systems and study techniques.

Each person is also born with **aptitudes** and talents. Some are artistic, some have a talent for communicating, and others have a flair for figures.

Example

The following are examples of ways in which an entrepreneur can use his or her aptitudes, expertise and skills in specific businesses.

Skills, expertise or aptitude	Types of enterprise
Technical thinking (aptitude) +	⇨ Draws furniture designs
Knowledge of antiques (expertise) +	⇨ Restores antique furniture
Cabinet-maker (skill)	⇨ Designs and installs kitchens and built-in cupboards
Artistic (aptitude) +	⇨ Produces and/or sells art
Experience in jewellery design (expertise) +	⇨ Designs jewellery
Apprentice in jewellery manufacture (skill)	⇨ Manufactures jewellery
Analytic, practical thinking (aptitude) +	⇨ Develops computer programs
Experience in stock control (expertise) +	⇨ Develops methods of stock control for enterprises
Knowledge of book retailing and of the need for reliable suppliers (skill)	⇨ Provides central distribution service for suppliers of books to retail shops.

Usually, your skills, expertise and knowledge are a product of your natural aptitudes, talents and interests. Someone who has a strong verbal aptitude, for example, will learn languages easily and so develop a sound knowledge of languages with further study. People who are artistic can practice art as a career or a hobby. They could, for example, paint or be a graphic designer. Further study would enable them to qualify as an architect or jewellery designer.

You can see how important it is for an entrepreneur to consider his or her skills, expertise and aptitudes when planning to start a business.

1.5.2 The important personal characteristics of entrepreneurs

Before we discuss the personal characteristics, you should note that expertise, skills and aptitudes in isolation do not guarantee a successful enterprise. To ensure success in your own enterprise, business aptitude and management skills are indispensable. The following example highlights the range of skills necessary to manage an interior design business.

Example

A successful interior decorator must have a thorough knowledge of materials, furniture styles and the use of space. Knowledge of various manufacturers and their products and services is also essential. Such a person must also be artistic and creative, with a feel for colour and dimensions to be able to furnish a room tastefully. These are the person's expertise and talents. The interior decorator must also maintain sound human relations, because he or she will deal with many different people (clients, employees, suppliers and the public) when the business is marketed.

Involvement in the business ensures that the entrepreneur will use his or her expertise and talents to offer clients the best possible service. This in turn ensures the success of the business.

Here now are the personal characteristics that warrant attention.

Perseverance

Entrepreneurs have confidence in themselves and their businesses and carry on in spite of setbacks, difficult situations and problems. They are able to take immediate decisions, but can also exercise patience until a task has been completed and a goal reached. They do not lose heart when they make mistakes or fail.

Successful entrepreneurs have an intense determination and a need to overcome obstacles, solve problems and complete a task. They are not intimidated by difficult situations.

Commitment to the business

Entrepreneurs dedicate all their skills, expertise and resources to establishing and building the business. They prove their commitment by:

- using their own money to establish the business
- taking a mortgage on a house
- working long hours in order to succeed
- accepting a lower standard of living and possibly earning little or no income from the business until it is successful.

Involvement in the business

Entrepreneurs are personally involved in their business and are aware of everything that is happening on all levels and in all sections of the business. They perform tasks themselves and communicate well with staff and others involved with the business, such as suppliers and clients. The example of the interior decorator reminds us of the importance of personal involvement.

Willingness to take risks

Entrepreneurs take calculated risks. This means that the risk related to a business opportunity must not be too great, for then the chance of success is not in the hands of the entrepreneur. They are not gamblers. The level of risk should not be too low either, as then exploiting the opportunity does not pose a challenge and is usually not as profitable. A risk factor that is too low implies limited profitability. A business opportunity with a low risk factor makes it easy to enter the market, but also raises the likelihood of competition. In the business world this consideration is called 'barriers to entry'.

Entrepreneurs usually try to reduce risk by finding investors to provide finance, making arrangements with suppliers to provide goods on consignment or persuading suppliers to accept special terms of payment, etc. The successful entrepreneur will carefully plan and consider each business opportunity.

Sound human relations

Entrepreneurs work closely with other people. They realise they cannot be successful in isolation and therefore motivate their employees and know how to build contacts to the benefit of their business. They know it is important to ensure long-term relationships and stay on good terms with suppliers, clients and others involved in the business.

Successful entrepreneurs realise the importance of business relationships. They have good relations with clients, see human relations as an important resource of the enterprise and regard long-term goodwill as more important than short-term benefits. Sound human relations has been identified as one factor that differentiates the 'successful' entrepreneur from the 'average' in developing countries (McClelland, 1986).

Successful as well as average entrepreneurs maintain good personal relations by, for example, using influencing strategies to develop business contacts and influential people to achieve their goals. They are able to persuade people to buy a product or service or to provide financing. They also make use of their capabilities, reliability and other personal or business qualities (McClelland, 1986).

Creativity and innovative ability

Creativity refers to a person's imagination and ability to think creatively. Creativity is the generation of new and useable ideas to solve any problem or use any opportunity. In the long term, an enterprise's success is determined by the degree to which good ideas are generated, developed and implemented. Creativity consists of people being open to new ideas and new approaches to the business and focussing on what can be done differently to ensure success in the business. In other words, effective entrepreneurs take the initiative to solve problems in a unique manner. Innovative ability refers more to the use of creative abilities to create something concrete. So it is logical that creative thinking, but especially innovative ability, is fundamental to starting a new enterprise.

Creativity distinguishes an entrepreneur from his or her competitors. Often it does not represent a radically new method, but it may be a method that satisfies a client's need in a better way.

Positive attitude and approach

Entrepreneurs learn from their setbacks and failures. They are realistic and accept that disappointments are inevitable, and are not discouraged when these occur. They are able to identify opportunities even in adverse and difficult situations.

All this indicates that entrepreneurs remain positive despite setbacks, failure and disappointment. This does not mean they do not sometimes feel dispirited when events are not favourable, but on the whole they deal positively with situations. We often read of entrepreneurs who have lost everything, sometimes more than once, only to start afresh. Success is achieved by using negative experiences positively and by learning from past mistakes.

Example

In this way, Henry Ford, father of the motor car assembly line and the first mass-produced motor car (the Model T Ford), twice started enterprises (both times building racing cars) that proved unsuccessful, before achieving success.

1.5.3 The important functional management skills of entrepreneurs

The management skills of an entrepreneur are an indication of how well the entrepreneur can perform important tasks or activities in a business. Related activities are grouped, and are known as the eight functions of a business. They are shown in Figure 1.2.

The functions are described in more detail in Chapter 2, and also in Chapter 6 where they are applied as part of setting up a business.

In this section, which is about you, the entrepreneur, we discuss your ability to perform specific activities in the enterprise. You must be aware of your strengths and weaknesses in terms of management skills in the various business functions so that you can apply or supplement them to build a successful enterprise.

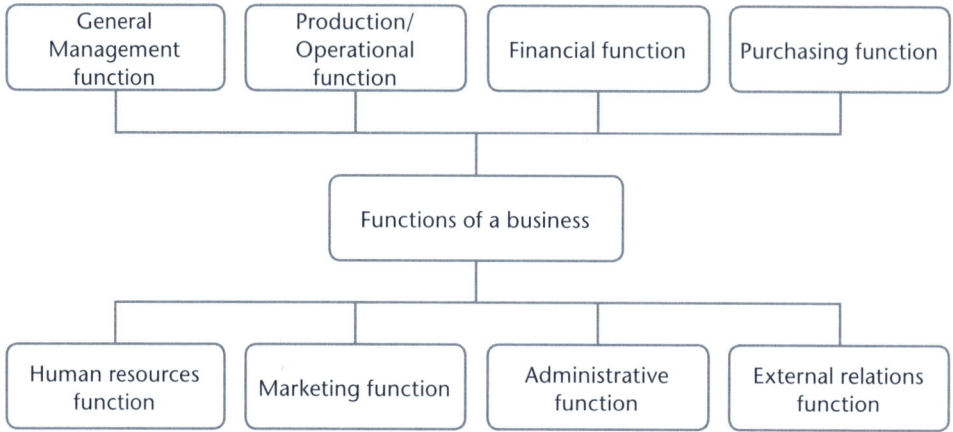

Figure 1.2: The eight functions of a business

If you think back to the example of the interior decorator, it is evident that the success of a business demands specific management skills.

Example

The interior decorator must be market oriented. She must know which target market is to be served, for example:

- the higher income group or corporate clients
- people with modern, traditional or alternative tastes.

The interior decorator must also be familiar with marketing methods and know how to reach the target market. Managing and applying the income and funds is equally essential for the survival and profitability of the business. If the interior decorator cannot manage her finances, she will have to get expert assistance.

According to management consultants, marketing expertise and management expertise are essential for the successful operation of SMMEs. To be successful, the entrepreneur should have a minimum or a particular combination of these management skills.

Important information

The following important aspects of management skills will be discussed below:

- planning a business before it is established
- general management skills and the use of advisers
- customer service
- knowledge of competitors
- market orientation
- the importance of quality products or services
- accounting for your own purposes
- insight into expenditure, income, profit and loss
- the ability to use income wisely.

Planning a business before it is established

This activity is part of the general management function and is part of drawing up the business plan. A well-considered business plan ensures that the business is launched with confidence, because it means the necessary research and planning has been done.

Entrepreneurs often do the planning very informally because there is no time to draw up a formal business plan, or because they simply do not know how to do it. Despite their informal planning, these entrepreneurs can be successful.

Important information

Formal planning and drawing up a business plan are desirable activities because they enable the entrepreneur to:

- identify problems early on so that he or she can make wise decisions and fewer mistakes
- consider all the important factors concerning the intended business and in so doing become less dependent on purely instinctive or crisis decisions, thereby avoiding stress
- take decisions for the future
- use this planning stage as an ideal opportunity for testing ideas.

A full discussion of, and guidance in, developing a business plan is given in Chapter 5.

General management skills and the use of advisers

This activity is also part of the general management function. Entrepreneurs must know what is needed for success in a specific business, and must be intent on developing their skills in these critical areas of performance. If marketing the business's products is the critical area of performance, and significantly determines the success of the enterprise, the entrepreneur must know how to carry out this function. If he or she does not have the necessary expertise, trained staff should be appointed. The entrepreneur should also understand the environment in which he or she is competing and be well organised. Know-how is often more important than creativity.

As an entrepreneur, it is logical that you will start a business in which you can use your expertise and skills (strengths). You will also usually be aware of, or soon discover, your weaknesses. Once you are aware of these, you can then strengthen or supplement your weak areas by:

- using other people, such as employees, consultants, contractors or professional experts
- working on your self-development and making conscious efforts to make up for deficiencies by learning from others, attending courses, reading or studying.

Example

The interior decorator knows that she is a very creative, artistic and stylish person. She realises that her financial knowledge is insufficient for her to do her own accounting, and so contracts this out to an accountant. As a good businesswoman she accepts that she must be able to understand financial statements, and so takes a course to learn basic financial terms and principles to be able to take proper business decisions. She has identified her weaknesses, and is taking steps to avoid having her enterprise harmed by them.

Customer service

This activity is included in the marketing and administrative functions. Entrepreneurs who maintain good human relations are sensitive to clients' needs, and so provide very good customer service. Examples are after-sales service; attention to details, such as serving refreshments when a client visits, personal presentability and attractive premises; user-friendliness, such as a neatly ordered shop and clear instructions for using products. Clients remember, support and recommend a business that meets their needs and gives them something extra without making them feel they are paying for it. Little gestures mean a lot: a balloon or sticker for the child; a cup of tea or glass of champagne in the jewellery store; changing an order on short notice; or just friendly, helpful service.

Administrative and technical factors are also crucial to sound customer service. Keep accurate records and an up-to-date filing system for reference and stock control. Use a diary so that you can plan your time and keep appointments, and job cards for client information. These are a few examples of methods to ensure effective customer service.

Knowledge of competitors

This activity is also part of the marketing function. Successful entrepreneurs know:

- who their competitors are
- how many competitors they have
- what size their competitors' operations are
- which segment of the market their competitors control
- what the quality of their competitors' products or services are
- how to distinguish themselves from their competitors and so ensure and increase their share of the market
- how to discover their competitors' strengths and weaknesses, and to convert a competitor's weakness into an opportunity for their own business.

Example

An example is an entrepreneur who sells Persian carpets, kilims and carrot cloths: he knows his competitors and distinguishes his business by visiting clients at home or at work. He takes along a variety of suitable carpets and cloths to make the client's choice easier. His professional know-how concerning the quality of the product and his taste and flair for colour (talent) are presented to the client in a unique fashion. He is successful because his competitors sell their products from their shops or at auctions, with no apparent interest in the client's home or place of work.

Market orientation

This activity is also part of the marketing function. Successful entrepreneurs are market-oriented. They know who their target market is, what the demands and needs of the target market are and how to meet them profitably. The example of the interior decorator illustrates this functional skill. A market-conscious entrepreneur has developed products and services to satisfy the client's requirements.

A market-conscious entrepreneur is positioned realistically towards competitors. This means that the entrepreneur's products and/or services are distinct from those of competitors to ensure profitability and a competitive edge. The customer is the focus of the business and products, and/or services are developed and adapted to meet the client's desires.

Product-oriented entrepreneurs often have problems because they are more concerned with the product than with the client, and consequently do not know how to market their products/services successfully.

The following quotation should serve as a warning:

Important information

'Many aspiring entrepreneurs are so in love with their product-service idea that they ignore the market; they assume it will sell. The market road is strewn with product-service ideas that were heavily—and many times cleverly—advertised and went bust' (Burch, 1986: 79).

The importance of quality products or services

This activity is part of the marketing function as well as the purchasing function. Quality products are not necessarily expensive products. However, the client expects the quality of the product to be in keeping with the price charged. Value for money is important. A successful entrepreneur aims to offer clients a quality product while still remaining profitable. Costs must be kept in check without affecting the quality of goods. Quality products and services contribute to marketing, as they generate new clients through personal recommendations by existing, satisfied clients.

Accounting for your own purposes

This activity is part of the administrative and financial function. Successful entrepreneurs realise that they must be able to understand their own accounting systems. Simplicity and usefulness are the most important features of such systems.

A simple system that suits the business is essential. The entrepreneur must understand what has to be done and why it must be done so that the information it provides can be properly utilised. If the size and complexity of an enterprise are such that the accounting cannot be done internally, a qualified person must be appointed to perform this function. The usefulness of the information provided by the accounting system is of cardinal importance because it allows the entrepreneur to make decisions on how to improve the management of the enterprise.

Insight into expenditure, income, profit and loss

This activity is part of the financial function. Successful entrepreneurs distinguish between income and profit. They realise that income must first be used to buy new stocks, to pay creditors, wages, salaries, tax and for current expenses. Only once this has been done can the entrepreneur determine what portion of the remaining income or profit can be ploughed back into the business and how much can be used for personal remuneration. The entrepreneur knows how to calculate profit and what it means to show a loss. He or she must know which costs are essential and understand the implication of increased expenses. This management skill is closely related to the next skill, namely the ability to use income wisely.

The ability to use income wisely

This activity is also part of the financial function. We discussed this management skill in the example of the interior decorator.

The successful entrepreneur exercises financial discipline and understands what to spend money on to ensure success. An expensive motor car conveys an image of success, or may offer convenience to a client. If this is important to the business, the entrepreneur may take the risk of buying the car. On the other hand, a successful entrepreneur will not waste money on unnecessary personal luxuries and status symbols.

Entrepreneurs must constantly take decisions on expenses. They must develop the ability to make the right decisions to ensure growth.

Important information

Examples of good decisions are:

- postponing the payment to a debt/creditor for as long as possible to keep cash available for a special offer on necessary stocks, which will enhance profitability
- applying profits within the business instead of on holidays, luxuries or a more expensive house
- using money wisely in departments or on products that will result in the greatest profitability for the enterprise.

Remember that although all management skills are important, few if any entrepreneurs have all the management skills necessary to run a successful business.

1.6 Dealing with external factors that affect entrepreneurship

External factors and circumstances also influence the way an entrepreneur will be able to exploit his or her potential. How you accommodate, deal with and even exploit external factors to your personal advantage is a measure of your entrepreneurship.

Important information

As an entrepreneur you must be aware of the following external factors:

Economic conditions

The entrepreneur must know how to adapt to fluctuating interest rates or declining levels of customer spending power.

Technological changes

The entrepreneur must keep up with technological developments and know how to exploit them to the benefit of his or her business.

Social and cultural forces

The entrepreneur must be able to identify opportunities for growth in market share following a rise in levels of education among large sections of the population.

➲

Political and legislative variables

The entrepreneur must realise the opportunities that arise after political adjustments and events.

Physical variables

The entrepreneur must keep abreast of the availability and price of resources, such as considering the use of alternative raw materials following price rises.

International forces

The entrepreneur who uses technologically advanced communication channels can, for example, expand to and even establish a business in another country.

These external factors are discussed fully in Chapter 2.

Skills, expertise, aptitude, personal characteristics and management skills determine the way a person will handle external factors. The relationship between a person's inherent attributes and external factors are crucial to successful entrepreneurship.

1.7   Summary

The importance of entrepreneurial business at all levels is essential to a country's economic development, wealth and employment creation. To a large extent this is dependent on the entrepreneur, who applies certain talents, skills and expertise in the start-up, development and growth of businesses. Entrepreneurial development is the origin of successful entrepreneurial activity, and although some are born entrepreneurs, it is possible to develop individuals to become entrepreneurs. This is where entrepreneurial education and training plays an important role.

All the success factors that have been discussed must be analysed in personal terms. This may discourage some potential entrepreneurs, but it is vital that the aspiring businessperson be aware of all the important aspects. Remember that a successful entrepreneur is critical of him- or herself, but positive about solving problems. The entrepreneur will therefore see which adjustments must be made or what can be done to start an enterprise that has been a dream. Thus the entrepreneur has a vision. He or she realises that it is essential to evaluate personal strengths and weaknesses realistically to achieve the goals.

Self-evaluation questions

1. Describe the entrepreneur and indicate how the entrepreneur differs from the small business manager.
2. What is the value of the entrepreneur to the economy of a country?
3. Identify an entrepreneur and describe what his or her business entails and why you regard the person as an entrepreneur. Also indicate whether you regard the business as a micro, small or medium enterprise. Motivate why you classify the business as such.
4. Determine how a medium business differs from a small business.
5. Discuss the importance of the skills, expertise and aptitudes of an entrepreneur and determine your own skills, expertise and aptitudes.

6. List the seven personal characteristics that may contribute to successful entrepreneurship.
7. List and briefly describe the eight functional management skills of successful entrepreneurs.

References and further reading

Bird, B J. 1989. *Entrepreneurial Behavior.* Glenview, IL: Scott, Foresman and Company.

Burch, J G. 1986. *Entrepreneurship.* New York: John Wiley and Sons.

Bygrave, W D, Reynolds, P D & Autio, E. 2004. *Global Entrepreneurship Monitor: 2003 Executive Report.* London: Babson College.

Centre for Development and Enterprise. 2004. 'Key to growth: Supporting South Africa's emerging entrepreneurs', *Research Report 12.* June. Johannesburg.

Department of Trade and Industry (dti). 2008. *Annual Review of Small Business in South Africa 2005–2007.* www.thedti.gov.za (accessed 7 April 2011).

Financial Mail. 2005. 'Business schools: Vital or useless? (Ranking the MBA's)', September 16.

Franchise Advice and Information Network (FRAIN). 2004. *Franchise Census 2004.* Pretoria: CSIR.

Johnson, D M. 2004. 'In the mainstream, multi-unit and multi-concept franchising', *Franchising World*, April.

Kao, R W Y. 1993. 'Entrepreneurship', *Journal of Creativity and Innovation*, 1(3): 69–71.

Kao, R W Y, Kao, K R & Kao, R R. 2002. *Entrepreneurism: A Philosophy and a Sensible Alternative for the Market Economy.* London: Imperial College Press.

Karl, K. 2000. 'The informal sector', *The Courier: Africa-Carribean-Pacific-EC*, 178, December/ January 1999–2000.

Ligthelm A A. 2004. 'Profile of informal microenterprises in the retail sector of South Africa', *Southern African Business Review*, 8(1): 39–52.

Loxton, L. 2005. 'Inside parliament: New law to boost close corporations', *Star Business Report,* June 20.

Maritz, P A. 2005. 'Entrepreneurial service vision in a franchised home entertainment system', unpublished BCom thesis (Business Management), University of Pretoria.

McClelland, D C. 1961. *The Achieving Society.* Princeton, NJ: Van Nostrand.

McClelland, D C. 1986. 'Characteristics of successful entrepreneurs', *Journal of Creative Behavior*, 21(3): 219–233.

Naudé, C. 2004. 'Wat SA se top entrepreneurs gemeen het', *Finansies en Tegniek*, April 7.

Nieuwenhuizen, C & Kroon, J. 2002. 'Creating wealth by financing small and medium enterprises of owners who possess entrepreneurial skills', *Management Dynamics: Contemporary Research*, 11(1).

Orford, J, Herrington, M & Wood, E. 2004. *Global Entrepreneurship Monitor: South Executive African Report 2004.* Cape Town: University of Cape Town, Graduate School of Business, Centre for Innovation and Entrepreneurship.

Schumpeter, J A. 1934. *The Theory of Economic Development.* Translated by R. Opic. Cambridge, MA: Harvard University Press.

South Africa. 2003. *National Small Business Amendment Act No. 26 of 2003.* Government Gazette, 461(25763), November 26.

Statistics South Africa. 2004. *Labour Force Survey.* Statistics South Africa, September.

Sunday Times Business Times. 2001. 'Diary of a retail revolutionary', November 11.

Theunissen, G. 2005. 'Informal economy: World Bank "wrong"', *Finance Week*, April 20.

Van Eeden, S, Viviers, S & Venter, D. 2003. 'A comparative study of selected problems encountered by small businesses in the Nelson Mandela, Cape Town and Egoli metropoles', *Management Dynamics*, 12(3): 13–23.

CHAPTER TWO

Basic business concepts and the business environment

Andreas De Beer

> ### Learning outcomes
>
> After you have studied this chapter, you should be able to:
>
> - explain the motivation for setting up a business
> - analyse the relationship between the business and its establishment
> - distinguish between the terms 'branch of industry' and 'production branch,' using examples to illustrate them and their use in classifying a business
> - arrange the three sectors in which businesses are grouped and provide suitable examples
> - draw an industrial column for a product to illustrate the route it follows—from the raw material stage, to delivery, to the customer
> - describe the micro environment of the business
> - explain the market environment and the variables which influence the business's growth and existence
> - identify the macro environment and all the forces and influences which affect the business.

We are going to look at two important concepts in this chapter: basic business concepts and principles, and the reason why the environment is so important in the business world.

The first part of this chapter will look at the enterprise as a need-satisfying organisation in the free-market system and show the relationship between the enterprise and the establishment. This section will clarify how entities are categorised into branches of industry and production. After the categorisation we will explain the different sectors of the economy in which these entities operate and describe how raw materials and products move through these sectors to reach the consumer. These are all 'basic business concepts'.

2.1 Introduction

Consider whether it is possible for a business to exist in total isolation. Ask yourself if it is possible for a business to grow and exist if factors such as the customer and his or her needs, competitor activity and prevailing economic and political conditions are not taken into consideration. The answer to these questions should be no: of course it is not possible for any business, large or small, to function in isolation. To be successful, a business must stay in constant contact with the market environment so that it remains up to date with changing customer needs, changing technology and competitor activities.

> ## *Example*
>
> A business manufactures long-playing records (LPs). Because of technological changes, most people today prefer CDs (compact discs) and DVDs (high-density video discs). What do you think will happen to this business?

Today's businesses function in an 'economy of ideas'. Never before in the history of business has so much change been introduced so quickly. Many of these changes are due to the changing business environment, in particular the rise of new communication technologies, multinational businesses and globalisation. The external and internal environment of every business is changing continuously and will affect every business.

Every business functions within an environment (the business environment) where events and variables influence its activities. These events may pose opportunities or threats. Technological development is a good illustration (think about the example above). On the one hand, technology offers opportunities because new products and services are created, while on the other hand, it can constitute a threat because it may result in products or services becoming obsolete.

> ## *Important information*
>
> As an entrepreneur, you must be aware of environmental variables and changes. With knowledge of these changes, you can develop a plan of action to deal with potential opportunities or threats. Without this knowledge, your business will not grow or may cease to exist.

It is also important that you understand some basic business concepts, such as the role your business (or proposed business) plays in a free-market system, how different entities are categorised into branches of industry and production, the different sectors of the economy and how raw materials and products move through these sectors to reach the customer.

2.2   The business

> ## *Definition*
>
> A **business** or enterprise can be described as an independent institution, established by an entrepreneur to make a profit by producing goods or providing services that satisfy customers' needs. Therefore, the entrepreneur identifies a customer need and creates a business to produce goods and/or provide services to satisfy that need. The motive for the entrepreneur's action is to make a profit. In both cases the entrepreneur and the customer benefit from the creation of the business; the customer is able to satisfy his or her needs, while the entrepreneur makes a profit.

2.2.1 *The relationship between the business and the establishment*

Definition

The **establishment** can be described as the place where inputs such as raw materials and other components are processed to produce a product or provide a service. Production activities take place in the establishment.

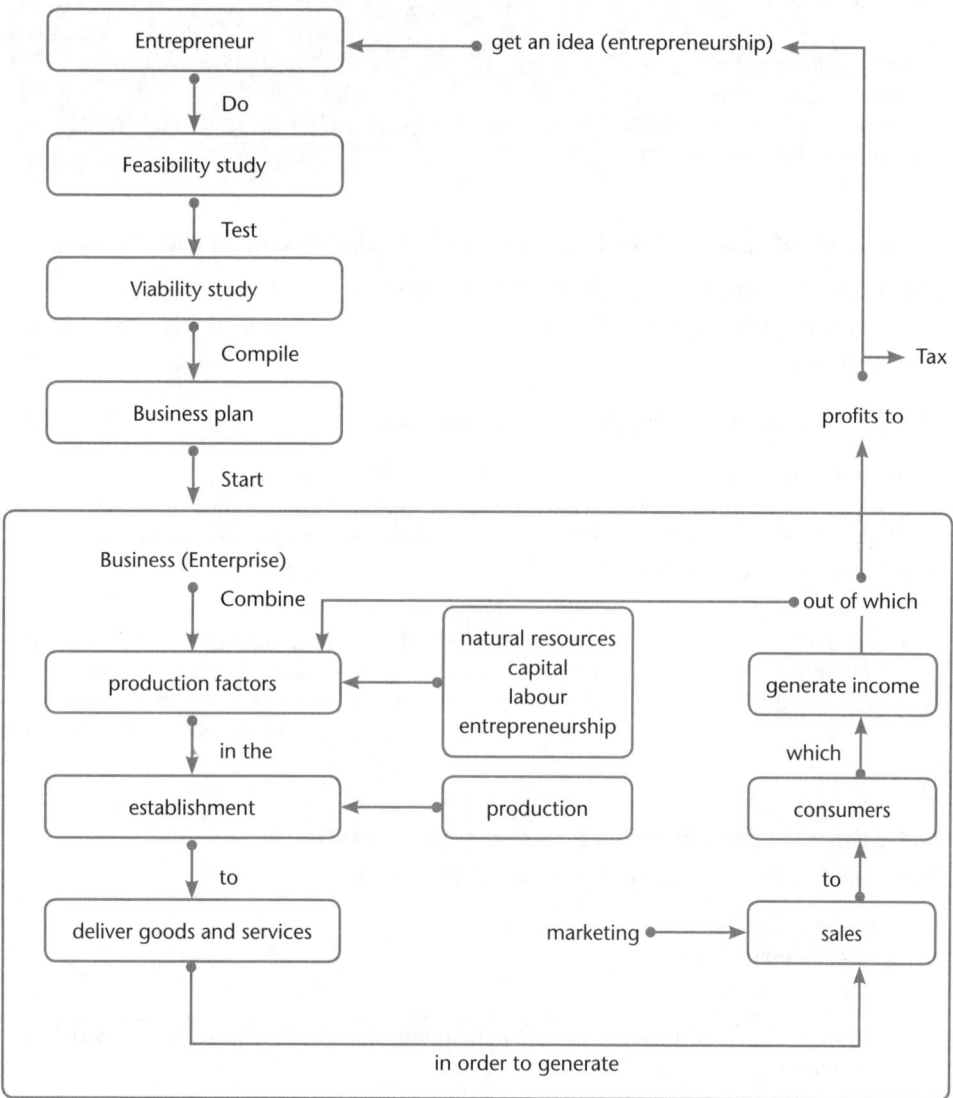

Figure 2.1: The relationship between the enterprise and its establishment

The best way of explaining the relationship between the business and the establishment is to look at Figure 2.1. This figure illustrates the shoe manufacturing business started by Tumi Lekoto (an entrepreneur). Tumi combines the production factors of natural resources, capital, labour and entrepreneurship in his business. Tumi (the entrepreneur) will employ people to work for him (labour). He will also buy (capital) the raw materials (natural resources) he needs to manufacture the shoes.

Once the production process is complete, the end product (shoes) can be sold using the marketing activities to generate income for Tumi's business. He will also use the external relations activities to improve the image of his business. The general management and administrative functions will oversee all the activities.

Important information

The establishment is a part of the business. The 'business' or 'enterprise' is the place where all the business functions take place (for example, marketing, management, administration) but the establishment refers **only** to the place where the product is made or the service provided.

2.2.2 Classification of a business and its establishment in the economy

The branch of industry and the production branch

The following table explains the difference between a branch of industry and the production branch.

Table 2.1: Branch of industry versus production branch

Branch of industry	Production branch
A branch of industry refers to all the businesses that produce more or less the same product or provide the same service. For example: The gold mines produce the same product—gold.	The production branch refers to all the businesses that use more or less the same production processes. For example: All the mines—gold, diamond and coal—form part of the mining production branch, because they all use the same production process, namely the extraction of natural resources through mining.

The different sectors in which a business can operate

There are three sectors in which a business can operate:

- the primary sector
- the secondary sector
- the tertiary sector.

The activities that take place in the establishment determine the sector in which the business operates.

- **The primary sector:** This sector is responsible for the exploitation of natural resources in their raw, unprocessed form.
- **The secondary sector:** In the secondary sector, the exploited natural resources are processed and transformed into products demanded by customers.
- **The tertiary sector:** This sector is responsible for distributing the final products from the manufacturer to the customer.

The industrial column

The diagram on the following page illustrates the industrial column, using the manufacture and distribution of paper as an example.

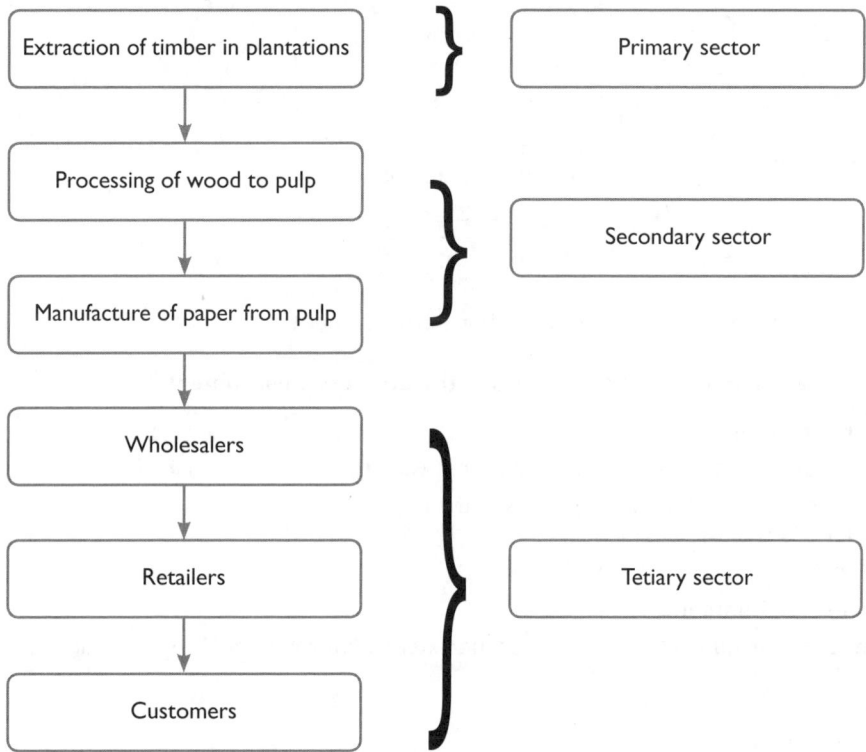

Figure 2.2: The industrial column

2.3   The business environment

The business environment is usually divided into three components, namely the micro (the internal environment), the market and the macro environments (both part of the external environment). These three components each have a variety of variables that can influence the business either positively or negatively. These are discussed in the following sections. Figure 2.3 gives an overall picture of the business environment. (The business is identified as the central point in this figure.)

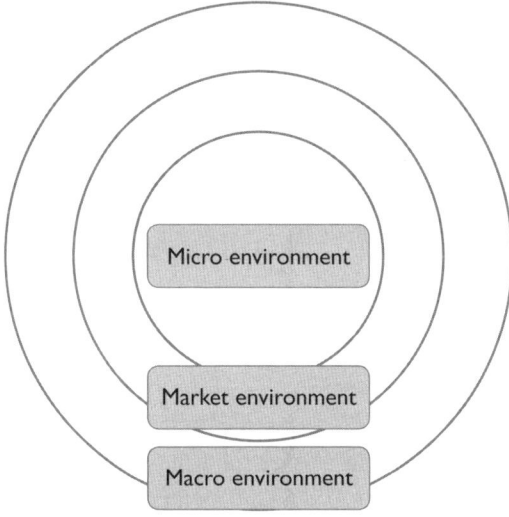

Figure 2.3: The internal and external business environment

Table 2.2: The components and variables of the business environment

The micro environment
This is the business itself. We can distinguish between the following variables: • the mission statement and objectives of the business • the functions of the business • the production factors of the business.
The market environment
This surrounds the business and is part of the external environment. The main variables include: • the market • the competition • the suppliers of resources and services (without which the business would not be able to manufacture and market its products and/or provide services).
The macro environment
The macro environment surrounds the market environment and the business. We can distinguish between the following sub-environments: • economic environment (economic conditions) • social environment • technological environment • physical environment • political and statutory environment • international environment.

2.3.1 The micro environment

The micro environment is the heart of the business. It indicates to what extent the business is able to utilise opportunities or oppose threats in the external environment.

Definition

The **micro environment** is the sum total of all the factors and variables which occur internally in the business and are influenced in a direct or indirect way by management decisions. These factors and variables have a fundamental influence on the establishment and on the growth and continued existence of the business.

What follows is a brief discussion of the three variables of the micro environment.

The mission statement and objectives of the business

This is what the business hopes to achieve and the way in which it can be achieved. The mission statement and objectives must correspond with the demands of the external environment.

The functions of the business

These include the following divisions that will be discussed in more detail overleaf:

- general management
- personnel management
- operations management
- purchasing management
- marketing management
- public relations management
- administrative management
- financial management.

Important information

General management: General management differs from the other functions in that it cannot be placed in a department on its own. General management concerns all the activities that are necessary to the very important task of management on all levels throughout the entire organisation.

Personnel management: Personnel management includes all the activities concerned with the procurement, development, compensation, integration and maintenance of the personnel of the organisation.

Operations management: This refers to the management process used in both manufacturing and service enterprises. Operations management can be described as those management activities that take place so that products and services can be provided to satisfy the needs of the consumer.

Purchasing management: The purchasing function deals with the procurement of all the resources an organisation needs to achieve its objectives. This includes, among other things, the determination of purchasing needs, the establishment of alternative suppliers who can satisfy these needs and the negotiation of agreements with them to the long-term advantage of the organisation.

Marketing management: Marketing is the process of transferring goods and services to customers in order to satisfy their needs, as well as the activities that make the transfer possible. Marketing therefore entails more than just advertising products and services; it includes a variety of activities cutting across all functions of the enterprise.

Public relations management: Public relations is the management function that evaluates public attitudes, identifies the policies and procedures of an individual or organisation with a public interest, and plans and executes a programme of action to earn public acceptance and understanding.

Administrative management: The administrative function can be defined as being concerned with the service of obtaining, recording and analysing information, and communicating the results to management who then can safeguard the assets, promote the activities and achieve the objectives of the organisation.

Financial management: Financial management refers to the management of the business's financial activities. The financial functions therefore include all the activities involved in obtaining capital and the efficient use thereof. The financial manager is responsible for the effective planning, organising and control of all the financial activities in the organisation.

The production factors of the business

These include the resources available to a business, such as labour, raw materials (such as minerals, timber and water), capital and entrepreneurship. With these resources the business must utilise opportunities to ward off threats in the external environment. For example, if a business has sufficient capital available, new markets and new products can be explored. On the other hand, a lack of capital may constitute a threat to the business because, unlike its competitors, the business is in a weaker position in the market.

The influence of management on the micro environment

As the manager of your own business, you will exert a direct influence on the mission statement and objectives of the business. You will decide where the business is going and what it will do to get there, and establish guidelines for its day-to-day operation.

2.3.2   The market environment

The market can be defined as the link between the business and the environment in which it functions. It surrounds the micro environment.

Definition

The **market environment** is the sum total of all the factors and/or variables which exist externally that cannot be controlled but can sometimes be influenced so that it will have a positive or negative effect on the growth and existence of the business.

The market environment is surrounded by the macro environment (see Figure 2.3). The market environment therefore does not exist in isolation but is in fact influenced by both the micro and macro environments. We can explain this interaction by means of the following examples:

Example

A new shampoo is introduced to the market. Customers prefer this new shampoo to the existing products (in other words, it is preferred to the competitor's products).

A company changes its credit and collection policy. This has an influence on the customer because, for example, some people may prefer to buy on credit, even if they know that the prices are inflated to provide for credit risks (the possibility of bad debts). Some customers may therefore prefer to buy clothes from a store such as Edgars, which offers credit facilities, rather than Erica Fashions, which does not.

The market environment is also influenced by the macro environment. During a downward trend in the economy, for example, customers have less money to spend on luxury items, which will lead to a reduction in the sale of luxury products, such as expensive dinner services, clothing and luxury cars.

Three variables are peculiar to the market environment, namely:

- the market
- the competition
- the suppliers of resources and services.

The market

Here we refer in an abstract sense to 'the market' which concerns the customer and his or her needs rather than the physical marketplace.

The business manufactures or buys products and/or provides services with the idea of selling these (to either individual customers or other businesses or institutions). However, before a customer can become active in the market, he or she must have financial means (money). These financial means can be used to acquire the available goods and/or services. The customer has to choose between different goods and services because he or she has limited financial means. It can also happen, however, that although the customer has the necessary financial means, he or she is not prepared to buy the available goods and services.

Important information

From the point of view of the business, the market therefore includes all individuals, groups or institutions who have specific needs for goods and services and who are prepared to use their available financial means to acquire them.

Example

- The market of a clothing shop such as Edgars includes all people with a need for clothing who are prepared to spend their money on the available articles. Their activities are therefore directed at satisfying their needs.
- The market of South African Airways includes all people with a need to travel domestically or internationally who have the financial means to pay for the air ticket. These people must therefore be prepared to spend money on an air ticket in order to satisfy a need (to travel).

➲

- Some manufacturing businesses trade only with wholesalers and retailers and not with the general public. Their market therefore comprises other businesses. For example, you cannot buy a writing pad directly from Sappi; you have to obtain it from a retailer who sells stationery. The retailer, in turn, has bought the writing pad from a manufacturer such as Croxley, who bought paper from Sappi.

Different segments of the market have been identified from this example. Here is a further breakdown:

- **The consumer market:** This market consists of the end-customers who carry out transactions in order to buy and consume items such as clothing, food or cars.
- **The industrial market:** In this market, goods and services are purchased and used for the manufacture of products or the provision of services to end-customers. As mentioned above, Croxley buys paper from a paper and pulp business such as Sappi in order to manufacture writing pads, envelopes and cards. A business that manufactures kitchen cupboards also utilises the industrial market when it buys pressed-wood panels from Sappi Novaboard to manufacture its products.
- **The re-sale market:** In this market, manufactured goods are purchased by businesses with the sole purpose of re-selling them to individuals or other businesses at a profit. Pick n Pay, for example, buys canned vegetables and fruit (such as Koo and All Gold) to sell at a profit to its customers.
- **The international market:** International markets exist outside the borders of a country and include all foreign customers, manufacturers, retailers and authorities. For example, European traders buy South African fruit on the international market.
- **The government market:** In order to provide services and carry out its functions, government and municipal authorities purchase a range of goods and services, such as:
  - furniture and equipment for use in government schools
  - system(s) to pay salaries to teachers, the police, government officials
  - fire-fighting equipment
  - medical supplies and services.

When discussing the market, we should not forget that the customer has certain rights. As an entrepreneur, you should be aware of these in order to keep abreast of customers' needs. Institutions such as the Customer Council focus on informing customers of their rights. We can summarise these as follows:

   The customer has the right to:

- **Be informed:** The customer should receive objective information about the available products and services. The business must not mislead or harm the customer by withholding information about a specific product. For example, the customer has a right to know the ingredients in a tin of canned food and whether it contains colourants or preservatives.
- **Exercise personal choice:** A variety of products and services are available on the market and the customer has the right to decide which product or service he or she is going to buy. For example, the customer has the right to choose between All Gold and Koo products.
- **Be heard:** The business must be geared towards listening to and responding to the customer's complaints and requests. For example, if a customer complains about poor service, the entrepreneur/manager should respond.

- **Protection:** The customer's safety is important and he or she should be protected against unsafe products, for example by the warning on cigarette packets.

The competition

Consider the variety of cars available today, as well as the number of dealers who sell these cars: this is competition. The choice between different products indicates that there is competition in the market.

Important information

Competition boils down to the fact that each business tries to convince consumers that its products and services are the best and that they should therefore buy from their business.

As an entrepreneur, you must be aware of competitor activity because the actions of competitors may constitute a threat to your business. You must be aware of new or improved products on the market. Therefore it is vitally important to be informed about the competition in the external business environment. You must know who your competitors are, where they are situated (the geographic distribution), the products they offer the market, the quality of the products, the specific markets they serve, what their share of the market is, their financial resources and their general image in the marketplace.

Over and above the fact that businesses compete with one another's products and services, we can also distinguish between the following types of competition:

The suppliers of resources and services

You must decide which products you are going to manufacture and market, the quantities you can produce and the capital necessary for the project. However, you will be dependent on other institutions in the external environment to carry out your activities because you will not necessarily have the raw materials to manufacture your products. You will therefore have to rely on external suppliers for many products or services.

Example

Here is an example of a business that manufactures wooden furniture, which shows how it interacts with the external environment:

- To manufacture its furniture the company must buy wood, tools, glue, nails and various other products. All of these must be bought from external suppliers.
- The business uses water, electricity, communication and other services. All of these must be bought from the external environment, such as Eskom for electricity and Telkom for communication services.
- The business must make use of a bank or other financial institution so that it can pay wages and salaries and pay suppliers. They may also need a loan at some stage, for instance if they want to expand and build new premises.
- The business decides to build a bigger factory. They must use the services of an external property broker to buy the land and external builders and contractors to build the new premises.

➲

- The larger factory needs additional staff. An external recruitment company is used to fill the new vacancies.
- Finally, the business must sell its furniture. To do this, they use an intermediary—in this case a wholesaler—who markets the product and sells it to a retailer (let us say Joshua Doore), who then sells the furniture to the end-customer.

2.3.3 The macro environment

The macro environment surrounds the business and its marketing environment. It is made up of a wide range of variables which can affect the business and its marketing activities, either positively or negatively.

Definition

The **macro environment** consists of all the variables and factors outside the business which have a positive or negative influence on the growth and continued existence of the business and which encourage or hinder the achievement of its objectives.

The individual business has no control over the macro environment or the variables which operate within it. For example, a business has no control over a rise in interest rates or a change in the exchange rate. However, these changes impact every business in some way.

The macro environment consists of a number of sub-environments which are usually described as 'variables' or 'forces'. Here we refer to economic, socio-cultural, political, technological, statutory, physical and international influences and forces.

What follows is a brief discussion of each of the sub-environments already identified.

Economic environment (economic conditions)

The economic environment is that part of the macro environment consisting of factors which influence the personal disposable income of the customer as well as his or her purchasing behaviour. (The term 'customer' is used here in its widest sense; it also includes other businesses.) The customer has limited financial means to satisfy all his or her needs and is therefore forced to make choices.

The customer's disposable income is influenced by many economic factors, for example interest rates and exchange rates, inflation, trade cycles and the economic growth rate.

Interest rates

An interest rate is an indication of the price at which money can be bought; in other words, the price at which money is available on the money and capital markets. If the interest rate is 20% per annum for a long-term loan of R100 000, this means that the borrower must pay R20 000 per year (20/100 x R100 000) to secure the loan of R100 000. This is therefore the price which the borrower must pay for the money he or she wishes to borrow.

A rise in interest rates usually results in a decrease in spending. If someone wants to buy a car, for example, he or she will have to pay more to borrow the money and, ultimately, pay more for the car. Suppose the buyer buys a car through hire-purchase financing and interest rates subsequently rise. This means that the buyer's monthly instalments will also increase and that he or she will pay even more for the vehicle. The bond on a home loan works in the same way; as soon as the interest rates rise, so do the monthly loan instalments. The opposite is also true.

Inflation

Inflation results in a continual rise in the prices of products and services. This has a depressing effect on the economy because the purchasing power of the rand, and therefore also the purchasing power of the customer, decreases as inflation rises. The customer is able to buy fewer products for the same amount because the value of the money has decreased as a result of inflation. Since the late seventies, South Africa has had to deal with the negative influence of inflation; in some years this has reached double figures.

Example

The influence of inflation is clear from the following examples:

- In 1980 we paid 30c for a loaf of white bread. Today we pay between R7,00 and R11,00 for the same loaf of bread.
- In 1980 we paid 76c for a dozen eggs; in 1985 we paid R1,31 and today we pay between R18,00 and R20,00 depending on the size and type.

Trade cycles

All economies are subject to certain cyclical changes. We can distinguish between different phases in the economic cycle, namely a period of prosperity, followed by a period of recession and depression and then a period of recovery. You should be aware of the phase through which the economy is moving as this influences the management, growth and continued existence of the business. Each phase makes its own demands on the business:

- During a phase of prosperity, the business (the marketing and production divisions) has the opportunity to manufacture and market new products. The business therefore has the opportunity to explore new markets and to expand its share of the market.
- In contrast, during a recession customers' disposable incomes are lower and they therefore buy less. This has a direct influence on the demand for products and/or services and therefore also on the growth of a business.
- During the recovery phase, the business must prepare itself for the economic growth that will take place and should, for example, pay attention to personnel training programmes, the development of new products and ways to increase its sales and therefore its income.

Social environment

The social environment is governed by the demographics of the population and social and cultural variables. We can distinguish between the following demographic variables, all of which have an impact on the market:

Size and composition of the population

- **Population growth:** The size and composition of the market are directly influenced by the population growth of the country. When considering the size of the population, remember that families have grown smaller over the past few years, and consider what effect this will have on future markets.

- **Market composition:** The market is made up of different ethnic groups.

Each group has a distinctive culture and lifestyle.

- **Changing role of women:** Women make up a large proportion of the labour force today. This has a direct impact on the market because the working woman has different needs from the homemaker. For instance, more working mothers means a greater demand for crèches and nursery schools; families with two incomes have a higher disposable income; the clothing needs of the working women differ from the homemaker; and, finally, working women usually spend more money on time-saving goods such as ready-made foods.
- **Life expectancy:** Life expectancy has increased as a result of better medical services and healthier lifestyles. This means that there are many customers over the age of 60, which presents definite marketing opportunities. For example, in the tourist industry there are many opportunities for travel agents to develop tour packages for this target group.

Geographic location

Markets in the metropolitan areas are larger and more concentrated, meaning that a wider variety of products and services can be marketed and sold in and around the cities. Urbanisation and the depopulation of the rural areas have a direct influence on the distribution of the market.

Development level of the market

In South Africa today great emphasis is laid on training. Customers are more informed, which means they know precisely what they want and therefore make greater demands on businesses. The customer is aware of, and stands up for, his or her rights. In order to continue to exist and grow, every business must focus on the needs of customers.

Other

Social and cultural forces from the macro environment, which must be considered, include the following:

- **Changing awareness:** The customer today is well informed about quality and available options. They are aware of environmental concerns and consider such aspects as whether the manufacture of products contributes to pollution or uses scarce resources.
- **Time:** In today's busy world, the customer does not want to spend too much time on shopping, and will look for products that are convenient and save time. Some examples include portable laptop computers that can be used while travelling, or the prepared foods mentioned earlier.

  A further example is the appearance of convenience supermarkets in residential areas; people returning home from work want to be able to buy essentials as quickly as possible. The convenience and longer opening hours of the smaller supermarkets in suburban areas satisfies this need. The same principle applies to one-stop shopping centres: everything the customer wants is available under one roof.
- **Healthier lifestyle:** The current trend towards fitness and a healthier lifestyle is a further force the business must be aware of. There is greater demand for natural foods (foods without colouring agents or preservatives) and an increased demand for products linked to fitness, such as bicycles, running shoes and gymnasium apparatus.

Technological environment

The technological environment includes all aspects which give rise to new or improved products and services being made available on the market.

Example

The microwave oven, today a common convenience appliance in the average household, did not even exist 30 years ago. This product is the result of technological development which gave many businesses the opportunity to add a new product to an existing product range.

New technological developments or improvements create definite opportunities but they may also constitute certain threats. For instance, the development of DVDs means that VHS or Beta video machines are no longer manufactured. Factories that used to manufacture VHS or Beta video machines have been forced to change their strategies. In addition, think of the continual changes in computer technology and the influence these have on banking, for example. New technologically improved products are constantly being introduced into the market.

If a business does not keep abreast of changes taking place on the technological front, it could soon find its products obsolete. Therefore, the wise entrepreneur/manager would do well to make provision for research and development.

Physical environment

The physical environment means the natural resources in the country, and incorporates the total management of these resources. Natural resources include gold, coal, diamonds, water, natural forests, etc. The natural beauty of the country can be included as this influences the tourist market. The following variables in the physical environment should be taken into consideration:

Limited and expensive resources

The world's natural resources are limited and must be managed carefully. Customers today demand that manufacturers recognise these limitations. This could also create opportunities in two ways:

- for the business to advertise its own environmentally friendly procedures and thereby attract customers
- for business opportunities—consider the following examples:

Example

- South Africa currently has problems with the supply of electricity. Many entrepreneurial opportunities arise from this—solar heating for water, power-saving light bulbs and wind generators.
- South Africa has limited water supplies. Suggestions for entrepreneurial opportunities include sprinkler systems using recycled water and toilets with the two-flush option.

Environmentalism and pollution

Industry is often guilty of air, water and noise pollution resulting from their manufacturing processes. The effects of this and the role played by industry in combating pollution are receiving worldwide attention. Manufacturing businesses can play a role by considering such issues as packaging. Packaging in plastic or glass is very convenient but has definite disadvantages for the environment.

Occassionally poisonous waste products, which are extremely harmful to water and plant life, flow into rivers. The mining of minerals sometimes elicits strong opposition from conservationists, for example the polemic regarding the mining of minerals in the Limpopo and Mpumalanga provinces and St Lucia area. The construction of roads can mar the natural scenery; for example, conservationists were strongly opposed to the building of a tar road alongside the Knysna lagoon in the southern Cape, where pollution from accidents of, particularly, oil tankers could potentially endanger the delicate ecosystem.

Political and statutory environment

The government of the day influences businesses through its fiscal and monetary policies. For instance, interest rates have a direct effect on net income; municipal rates affect property tax, and of course the annual budget influences the total economy of the country. The budget is a useful document to study because it gives details of likely future spending and of how income will be generated. Some of the government's income is obtained from taxes paid by individuals and businesses.

Variables which influence the individual business include the following:

Statutory provisions

There are various statutory provisions with which businesses must comply. For example, every business must:

- have a trading licence before it can operate
- register as a taxpayer at the local Receiver of Revenue
- comply with statutory provisions when concluding contracts
- comply with municipal health requirements if it is involved in the food industry.

There are some recent developments with regard to the new Companies Act which came into effect 1 May 2011. The two most important changes are:

- The new Consumer Protection Act (CPA) as of 1 April 2011, which will be implemented by the National Consumer Commission (NCC), taking over from the Department of Trade and Industry's Office of Consumer Protection (OCP).
- The establishment of the Companies and Intellectual Property Commission (CIPC) as of 1 May 2011. CIPC will register companies, promote awareness of company and intellectual property law, and monitor compliance of financial reporting standards.

Chapter 4 will discuss these changes in more detail.

Trade unions

Every business has a responsibility towards its employees. There are various laws which help to maintain a smooth relationship between the employer and employee. Although statutory provisions and regulations protect the rights of the employee, the existence of trade unions is an important variable in the macro environment. The voice of individual employees can easily be ignored by management.

Trade unions fight for the rights of workers who are in the same branch of industry. The employee acquires bargaining power through the trade union, which enables him or her to negotiate, for example, for higher salaries or better working conditions. In other words the trade union's main function is to negotiate on behalf of its members. Trade unions also defend and advance workers' rights and working conditions. In South Africa there are numerous trade unions, for example trade unions for mine workers, the motor industry, the steel industry and bank officials. If disputes are not resolved or are unfairly resolved, the Labour Relations Act of 1995 has made it possible to refer such cases to external mechanisms, such as the Commission for Conciliation, Mediation and Arbitration (CCMA).

Associations and institutes

In the same way as trade unions look after the interests of organised labour, many business associations and institutes campaign for the interests of businesses in their fields. Earlier on in this chapter we emphasised that a business has little, if any, influence over the macro environment. By means of associations and institutes, a business can promote its interests in the branch of industry in which it functions if it works with other businesses in the same branch of industry.

The following institutes and associations are well known and active in the macro environment:

- Afrikaanse Handelsinstituut (AHI)
- The South African Chamber of Business (Sacob)
- The Chamber of Mines
- The Motor Industries Federation.

International environment

We have seen that the variables influencing individual businesses originate from the local sphere (the business itself) and the national sphere (the market and macro environments). Over and above all these forces, the business must also still keep abreast of variables operating in the international sphere. These influences originate in the environment outside the country's borders and include the following:

International technology

South Africa is technologically developed in certain areas, such as in the fields of synthetic fuels, mining and veterinary science. However, South Africa also imports technology from other countries, for example computer technology from America and engineering technology from Germany and Japan. This is a phenomenon common to all developing countries.

International politics

South Africa felt the effect of international politics with the trade sanctions imposed in the mid-1980s. The country did not have access to foreign loan capital, for example, and this had a negative effect on the economic growth rate and job creation.

International economy

Economic factors and variables such as interest rates, exchange rates, the gold price, the economic growth rate, inflation, the availability of capital and a scarcity of resources occur worldwide and influence the economic conditions of all countries. For example, think of the effect inflation has had on the economies of Zimbabwe, Russia and Argentina. Amongst other things, high inflation rates resulted in very high food prices in these countries.

The rand–dollar and dollar–euro exchange rates have a significant influence on South African import and export activities. If the rand–dollar exchange rate is weak, the cost of importing goods becomes higher for a South African business. An example of this is the cost of overseas textbooks, which are currently expensive because the rand–dollar exchange rate is unfavourable for South African booksellers.

2.4   Summary

It is quite impossible for any business to function in total isolation. Without interaction with the business environment achieving your objectives will remain a dream and your business will not continue to grow and may even cease to exist.

You must continually gather information to analyse trends in the market. From this information, you can analyse potential opportunities and threats. The business environment offers opportunities which help you to achieve predetermined objectives. The opposite could also be true: if you do not heed important signals in the business environment, it could lead to potential closure of your business.

Remember also that the different components of the business environment, as identified, are not independent of each other. There is constant interaction between the different sub-environments.

Self-evaluation questions

1. With the aid of a practical example, illustrate the relationship between the business and the establishment.
2. Discuss the three sectors in which businesses and establishments can be grouped, and motivate your discussion with practical examples.
3. Draw your own industrial column for the production of wine.
4. Explain the meaning of the concept 'business environment' and identify the most important characteristics of this environment in your explanation.
5. Give reasons why a business cannot grow and continue to exist in total isolation.
6. Name three components of the business environment and give a description of each.
7. Discuss the micro environment and its variables.
8. Identify the variables in the market environment and discuss each one.
9. With the help of examples, discuss the different markets in which a business manufacturing wooden furniture can conduct business transactions.
10. Identify your rights as a customer and illustrate each right with the aid of a practical example.
11. Explain the meaning of 'competition'. Illustrate your answer with practical examples.
12. Do you think it is necessary for the business to take the macro environment into account? Give reasons for your answer by discussing the different variables within the sub-environments.

13. Suppose you are the owner of a business which manufactures and markets wooden kitchen cupboards. Evaluate your business environment on the basis of the variables in the micro, macro and market environments.
14. Martha Mabuso is the owner of a business which sells computer equipment. She realises that she must take the variables in the external environment into account. However, she focuses only on the variables in the market environment and does not consider those in the macro environment. Explain to Martha, with the help of suitable examples, which variables can be identified in the macro environment and what influence these may have on her business.

References and further reading

Bateman, T S & Scott, A S. 2002. *Management Competing in the New Era,* 5th ed. New York: McGraw-Hill.

De Beer, A A & Rossouw, D. 2005. *Focus on Operational Management: A Generic Approach.* Cape Town: Juta.

Hellriegel, D, Jackson, S E, Slocum, J, Staude, G, Amos, T, Klopper, H B, Louw, L & Oosthuizen, T. 2004. *Management.* Cape Town: Oxford University Press.

Nieuwenhuizen, C (ed). 2011. *Basics of Entrepreneurship,* 2nd ed. Cape Town: Juta.

Nieuwenhuizen, C & Rossouw, D (eds). 2008. *Business Management: A Contemporary Approach.* Cape Town: Juta.

CHAPTER THREE

The identification and development of business ideas

Hannelize Jacobs

Learning outcomes

After you have studied this chapter, you should be able to:

* identify the stages of setting up a business
* define creativity
* determine your own level of creativity
* improve the creativity of a team by using various creativity techniques
* creatively generate business ideas using structured methods/techniques
* distinguish between non-feasible and feasible ideas
* develop and refine a business idea.

Example

An example of a feasible business idea

Meeting the need to buy traditional South African products conveniently

In the early 1980s a small group of friends joined up to develop a new kind of home industry business concept in South Africa. They envisaged this home industry business to consist of a collective of entrepreneurs who prepare and spice up traditional and innovative homemade products and share a business premise from which to sell their products. At that time, this concept was an entirely new business idea in South Africa born out of the social needs of a group of young married women who wanted to earn an income and have a career like their husbands, while staying at home looking after their families. The name chosen for the new home industry business was 'Koljander', which is the Afrikaans word for the spice coriander, famous for its appetite-stimulating properties. Koljander sells a variety of quality traditional homemade eats and treats, and stocks top South African teas and coffees as well as exquisitely handmade crafts and cultural gifts. Clients buy directly from the shop, place orders and make reservations. Services include catering for weddings, functions and special occasions and a delivery service. Koljander's products meet the needs of customers who choose the convenience of buying traditional South African products, instead of making products themselves, at an outlet near their homes. Many of the co-operative members of the Koljander business involve family members, friends and domestic helpers in their production processes, creating additional job opportunities to contribute to the prosperity and well being of families and the community.

These micro entrepreneurial entities produce homemade goods as a 'family' or social unit drawing on the combined knowledge, skills and personalities of a diverse group of individuals. This innovative business concept is currently a common feature in South Africa, providing self-employment to hundreds of thousands of people. In almost every shopping mall in South Africa nowadays one can find a business based on a similar business idea and following the South African slogan 'local is lekker', meaning local is great.

Adapted from an article written by Hannelize Jacobs and Natasha Mwila (2011)

3.1 Introduction

Setting up a business can be divided into three main stages, namely:

- the identification of a feasible and viable business idea (the idea stage)
- the drawing up of a business plan (the planning stage)
- the implementation of the business plan (the implementation stage).

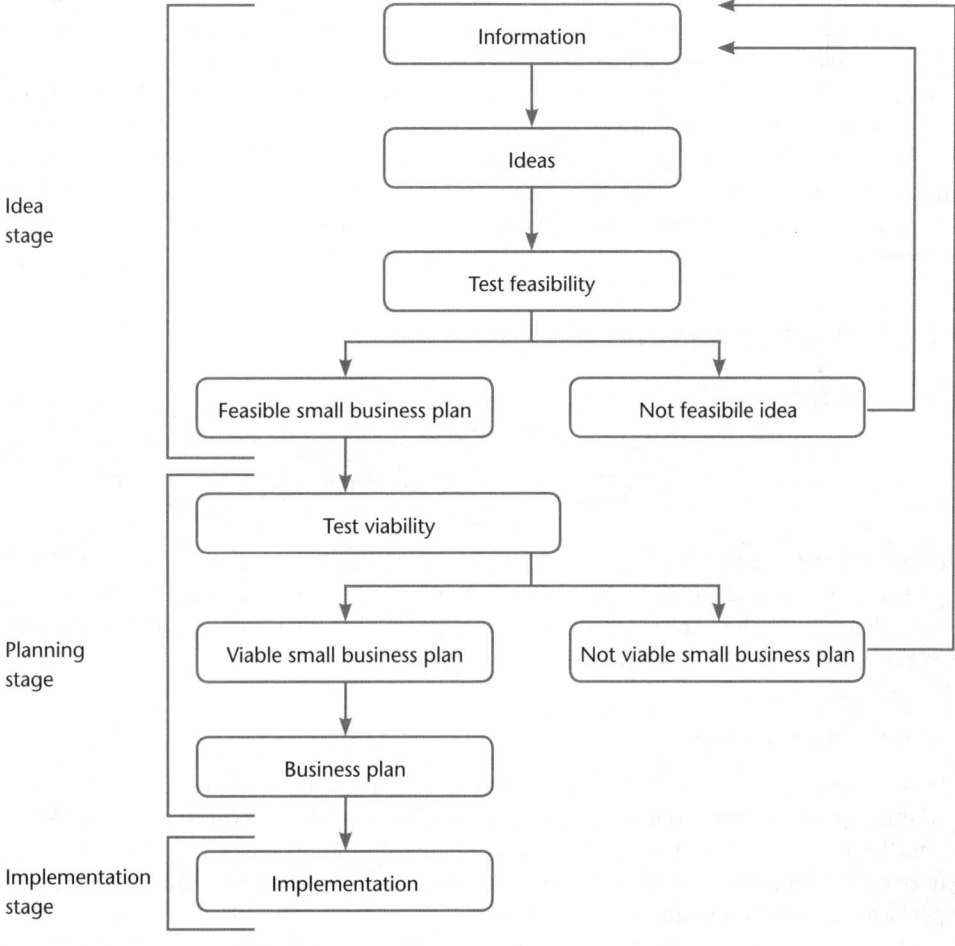

Figure 3.1: The three stages involved in setting up a business

Figure 3.1 illustrates this three-stage process.

These three stages form the theme of the rest of the book. In this chapter we will discuss the first stage, namely the identification and development of business ideas. Chapters 4 and 5 deal with the planning stage and Chapter 6 looks at the implementation stage.

The identification of business ideas is a creative process. As a potential entrepreneur, you must therefore be able to assume a creative attitude. All of us have the potential to think creatively. In this chapter you will be introduced to certain techniques which can be used to improve your creative mindset.

Although it is important to think of as many business ideas as possible, only one idea can eventually be converted to a business enterprise. This chapter will help you to identify a suitable idea (ie a feasible and viable business idea).

3.2   Cultivating a creative attitude

Chapter 1 explained that the capacity to act creatively and innovatively is one of the personality traits of an entrepreneur (turn back to page 10). Although a new and innovative business idea can be very satisfying, it can be very difficult to establish because it is not always easy to be first with a new product or service. When you are first, you must convince people that there is a need for your product or service. On the other hand, being second or third means that you can learn from the mistakes of others.

This does not, however, imply that you should imitate others directly and offer the market something identical. As an entrepreneur, you should try to provide specialised or exceptional products or services. You must think, therefore, of an idea(s) that will distinguish you from other competitive businesses. To do this you must think and act creatively.

3.2.1   What is creativity?

> **Definition**
>
> Being **creative** is generating a variety of really different ideas.

In order to be creative, you need to be able to view things in new ways or from fresh perspectives. Among other things, you need to be able to generate new possibilities or new alternatives. Tests of creativity measure not only the number of alternatives that can be generated but the uniqueness of those alternatives.

3.2.2   Am I creative?

How do we recognise creativity? Think of half a dozen people you believe to be creative; whether people around you or perhaps famous South African inventors such as Mark Shuttleworth, who invented an electronic security system, and Chris Barnard, who developed surgical procedures for organ transplants, invented new heart valves and performed the first human heart transplant.

What characteristics or abilities do these people have in common which make them creative? Note down a dozen that they all share. Obvious abilities with which you could start your list might include:

- solving problems in a different way
- thinking imaginatively
- seeing possibilities others have not seen
- initiating change.

The creative person usually enjoys problem-solving and tends to bring fresh perspectives to old problems. Here are some fun problems to stimulate creativity.

Example

You are participating in a race. You overtake the second person. What position are you in?

Answer: If you answered that you are first, then you are absolutely wrong! If you overtake the second person and you take his place, you are second!

If you overtake the last person, then you are…?

Answer: If you answered that you are second to last, then you are wrong again. Tell me, how can you overtake the last person?

Two Russians walk down a street in Moscow. One Russian is the father of the other Russian's son. How are they related?

Answer: They are husband and wife.

```
• • •
• • •
• • •
```

Join these nine dots (3x3) with not more than three lines

Answer: There is often more than one right answer to a problem. This problem can be solved in, among others, the following ways:

- If you take a thick pencil, you could join the dots with just three lines.
- If you take a very thick pencil, you can do the job with just one line!
- By rolling the paper into a cylinder you could draw one long line which encircles the cylinder.
- You can fold the paper in three, so the rows of dots all line up, and fold it again and poke the pencil through.

Make four triangles, all the same size with only six matches.

Answer

Creative thought can be divided into divergent and convergent reasoning.

Definition

Divergent thinking is the intellectual ability to think of many original, diverse and elaborate ideas.
Convergent thinking is the intellectual ability to logically evaluate, critique and choose the best idea from a selection of ideas.

Both of these abilities are necessary for creative output. Divergent thinking is a thought process used to generate ideas by exploring many possible solutions, whereas convergent thinking is a thought process used to organise and structure the many solutions to arrive at one best solution.

Research has shown that divergent (creative) thinking is natural for right-brain dominant people, whereas convergent (logical) thinking is natural for left-brain dominant people. The right brain processes data in a rapid, complex, whole-pattern and perceptual manner, while the left brain operates in a more verbal, analytic mode.

Brain hemispheric dominance can therefore be an indication of creative ability. Try to test your brain dominance with one or more of the online brain dominance tests, for example at www.puzzle.dse.nl/tests/index_us.html.

Although some people are born with the gift of creativity, it is possible for all of us to develop and improve our creative abilities. It is important to understand that creativity is just as much an attitude as a manner of thinking. It is thus possible to think of new ideas by attuning yourself to creativity. Use the following methods to improve your creativity:

- **Actively seek ideas:** You can learn to seek ideas actively by judging everything that you read or observe on the strength of the ideas that can be developed from it. If you think in this way regularly, it will become a habit and ideas will come to you more easily.
- **Write your ideas down:** Make a habit of writing down an idea as soon as you have one, even if you feel it is not a good idea. Regularly read through the ideas. This will give you the opportunity to review them and perhaps combine them in a new concept.
- **View a topic from another person's perspective/point of view:** Put yourself in somebody else's position to get a different perspective on a topic. With a better understanding of other people's points of view, you will gain new insights and ideas. By asking yourself, for example, what the mother of a pre-school child thinks of the concept 'to see red', and then looking at the same idea from the perspective of a busy businesswoman or a widowed grandmother, you can generate totally new ideas.
- **Break your routine:** A good way of stimulating your thoughts is to break your routine. Here are a few suggestions:
  - Take note of how you perform everyday actions, such as washing the dishes, and then do them differently.
  - Spend a whole day without something that is a part of each day's routine, for example your cellular phone.
  - Browse the web on a subject that you know nothing about.
  - Start a conversation with a stranger (someone you would not normally speak to).
  - Do something you have never done before, such as going to the theatre, riding a horse or starting a new hobby or sport (in other words, broaden your horizons).

- **Explore the grey areas:** If you tend to see only the right and wrong sides of a case, it is time to explore the grey areas between right and wrong. Make a habit of looking for different solutions and possibilities. Start by completing the following incomplete questions. See how many solutions you can find to each in ten minutes.
  o What will happen if I ...?
  o In what different way can I ...?
  o Who will benefit by ...?

Take some time to tune your mind for creativity before you start looking for business ideas. This mindset will eventually help you to identify new or better business ideas.

Team creativity

There are at least 200 different techniques and tools to enhance the creativity of teams, for example:

- Brain sketching
- Card story boards
- Bunches of bananas
- Pin cards
- Trigger sessions
- Brainstorming
- Creative problem solving (CPS)
- Idea advocate
- Superheroes
- Visualising a goal.

Some of these are discussed here.

- **Brain sketching:** With this technique you pass evolving sketches around the group. Limited facilitation skills are required.
  o A group of 4 to 8 people sit around a table, or in a circle of chairs. They need to be far enough apart to have some privacy. The problem statement is agreed and discussed until understood.
  o Each participant privately draws one or more sketches (each on separate sheets of paper) of how it might be solved, passing each sketch on to the person on their right when it is finished. The facilitator suggests that sketches should not take more than five minutes to draw.
  o Participants take the sketches passed on to them and either develop or annotate them, or use them to stimulate new sketches of their own, passing the amended original and/or any new sketches on to their neighbour to the right when ready.
  o After the process has been running for a suitable period and/or energy is running down, the sketches can be collected.
  o It will probably help to display all the sketches and to discuss them in turn for clarification and comments.
  The team then moves on to any appropriate categorisation, evaluation and selection process.
- **Bunches of bananas:** The bunches of bananas technique is one of lateral thinking, reducing excessive left-brain attention (which may be fuelling a certain mindset). There are people who instinctively liven up a sluggish meeting by being provocative, or 'throwing in a bunch of bananas'. Here are some tips:
  o Consider the mood and atmosphere: are there signs of the group being stuck in a rut, sluggish or showing inertia?
  o What could you say or do to assist the group out of this state of inertia?
  Create 'bunches of bananas' to suit your own character and style.

- o Bear in mind that you are engaging in a 'whole-brain' activity. Just as with a comedian, it is as much the delivery as the idea that brings about the effect.
- o If the group is inexperienced, the approach may have to be appropriately signalled: 'I know this is going to sound a little crazy, but bear with me. Sometime you can get out of a rut in the most unexpected ways ... .'
- o 'Bunches of bananas' can come in a variety of forms—any well-placed joke or image that captures attention when appropriate.

Example

For example, a group wanting to market goods from the United Kingdom to Australia exhausted all the obvious possibilities and seemed to be 'stuck'. Then someone said:

'We don't seem to be getting very far. What I'd like to do would be to find a product that every Australian sheep would be clamouring to buy'.

Although this comment could have been met with disapproval or polite silence, the timing of his 'Bunch of Bananas' was just right and someone picked up the idea:

'Sheep? Oh, you mean for us to find large numbers of customers who can be influenced easily. Perhaps we have been concentrating too hard on too few clients'.

The discussion this idea triggered eventually led to a new product being marketed to Australia.

- **Superheroes:** Superheroes is a fantasy-based technique. Participants pretend to be a fictional (or real) superhero (Superman, the Incredible Hulk, Batman, James Bond, Wonder Woman, Sherlock Holmes, Spiderman, etc) and use their 'super' characteristics to trigger ideas.

  This technique is good for creating an atmosphere of light-hearted fun in which energy is high and fantasy and metaphor are acceptable. All superheroes have skills and capacities that are outside 'normal' behaviour. This means that (a) people tend to think outside of the norm; and (b) play a role which allows them to express more unusual ideas than they might not normally express.

  Superhero stories also have strong elements of wish-fulfilment and can therefore help people to express wishes. It may not be suitable for very serious or introverted groups, or where there is a lack of trust.
  - o Prepare some general information on each superhero in advance. This could include their name, special powers, weaknesses, background, picture, etc. You can also provide props if you have an extrovert in the group.
  - o Display and discuss the problem to ensure everyone understands the issue. It can be useful to use brainstorming to list the more obvious ideas. (Brainstorming is a technique to allow people to build on each other's ideas. Members of the group put forward ideas without interruption or evaluation from the others.)
  - o Select a superhero for each participant. (Participants could also choose one for themselves, or take one from your information pack.) Get them to think a little about that superhero and talk to them about what life is like as a superhero in order to help them get into the role.

- The superhero characters are then used as the basis of an excursion, from any viewpoint. The extrovert groups will get into the role ('I will heat the chemicals instantly with my laser eyes whilst freezing the container with my breath'), whereas the more introverted groups will tend to be happier talking in the third person ('Superman could heat the chemicals with his laser eyes ...').
  - Start by getting each superhero to voice a few ideas.
  - Allow the group members to trigger off each other's ideas. Perhaps if Superman and Wonder Woman worked together they could produce an improved solution?
  - When you have sufficient ideas, evaluate them.
- **Trigger sessions:** Trigger sessions are a good way of getting lots of ideas from untrained resources.
  - The person with the problem explains and defines it.
  - Each member of the group writes down his or her ideas quickly (two minutes only).
  - One member reads out his or her list—others silently cross out ideas that are read out and write down ideas that are 'hitch-hiked' (ideas that are triggered by the ideas that are read out).
  - The second member reads out his or her list (ideas not covered on anyone else's list), followed in turn by other members.
  - The last member reads out his original list plus his 'hitch-hiked' list. The procedure is then repeated in the reverse order to the original order (for example, if there are six members, the order is: member 1, 2, 3, 4, 5, 6, then 5, 4, 3, 2, 1, then 2, 3, 4, 5, 6 etc).

A good group will be able to manage several passes. Everyone's paper is then collected and can be typed up into a single list of ideas—all duplicates should have been crossed out during the session.

3.3 Generating business ideas

A good business idea seldom comes out of the blue or as an inspiration. As a potential entrepreneur, you must deliberately look and think creatively for ideas that can be converted into a business.

In your search for ideas, you can make use of certain structured techniques. The techniques for the generation of business ideas proposed in this book can be divided into five broad approaches:

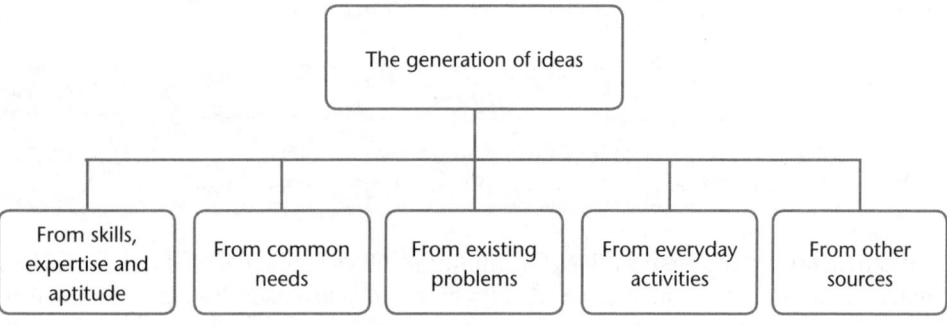

Figure 3.2: The generation of business ideas

These approaches have been tested successfully and promise to produce positive results. We will discuss them in the following sections.

3.3.1 The generation of ideas from the entrepreneur's skills, expertise and aptitude

We all have certain skills. In Chapter 1 we saw that an entrepreneur's skills, expertise and aptitudes are some of the key factors for success (turn back to page 8).

In addition, consider the following:

- Formal training does not necessarily guarantee success in a business enterprise. This does not mean that your qualifications are useless, however. Through your studies you can obtain certain knowledge that can lead to a business idea. An engineering student has, for example, gained certain technical knowledge which could give him or her the idea to start a specific manufacturing business.
- Skills can also be gained from working experience. As an employee you are responsible for certain activities. Your knowledge of these activities can enable you to start a business of your own involving these activities. For example, the fact that you functioned in a marketing capacity can be the reason why you want to start an advertising agency or act as a marketing consultant.
- Have you developed any skills through your hobbies or other non-career activities that could be used as ideas for your own business? For example, the fact that you collect comic books and know how to negotiate to get the best swap or price for your books means you have learned certain purchasing and negotiating skills.

Important information

Draw up a profile of your own abilities.

1. List your skills. For example, can you weld or knit?
2. Identify your expertise. List your formal qualifications (for example, diplomas or certificates), and experience gained (for example, handling difficult customers).
3. Write down your natural aptitudes/talents and interests. For example, you may be able to communicate well (this is an aptitude). Your interests may be woodwork or building websites.

This list of skills, expertise and aptitudes can now be used to identify business ideas. To show you how this can be done, consider the following example:

Example

Sarah Qubeka has one outstanding skill, namely that she can cook well. With this skill she can provide a product or service for individuals or organisations.

You can identify many business ideas by thinking of how to provide products or services to individuals or organisations, and what types of products or services they might need.

By doing the exercise on the following pages, you can see how many ideas Sarah, with her single skill, could identify.

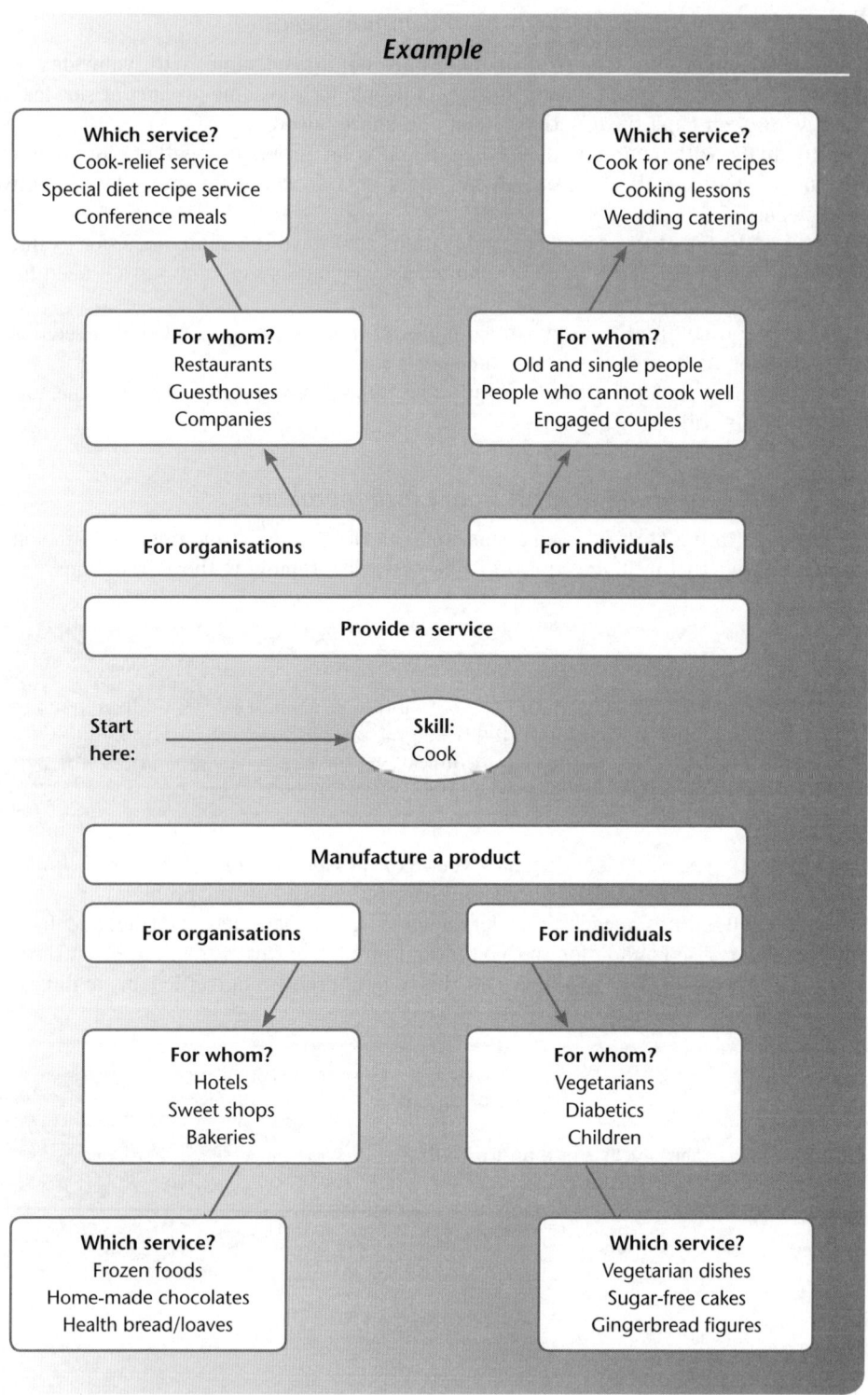

Example

Which service?		Which service?
Cook-relief service		'Cook for one' recipes
Special diet recipe service		Cooking lessons
Conference meals		Wedding catering

For whom?		For whom?
Restaurants		Old and single people
Guesthouses		People who cannot cook well
Companies		Engaged couples

For organisations   **For individuals**

Provide a service

Start here: → Skill: Cook

Manufacture a product

For organisations   **For individuals**

For whom?		For whom?
Hotels		Vegetarians
Sweet shops		Diabetics
Bakeries		Children

Which service?		Which service?
Frozen foods		Vegetarian dishes
Home-made chocolates		Sugar-free cakes
Health bread/loaves		Gingerbread figures

Now take one of your skills and do a similar exercise.

3.3.2 The generation of ideas from common needs

We all need something. However, our needs are not all the same. With your idea, you should try to satisfy a need among a range of people for the same product or service. In other words, you must try to satisfy a common/shared need.

Individuals with common needs can usually be grouped together, for example all mothers with small children, all members of a soccer team and all prospective homeowners.

You can also identify groups of organisations that have the same need, for example businesses that need catering on a regular basis, or businesses that have a need for a complete maintenance service.

Try this yourself and write down examples of interest groups and their needs on a sheet of paper. An example is given on page 49.

By concentrating on the needs of only one interest group, you will find that many business ideas will occur to you.

3.3.3 The generation of ideas from existing problems

Instead of thinking of unfulfilled needs, you can think of existing, unsolved problems. Think of things that irritate you. Now think of ways of removing those irritations.

Example

Small businesses can usually only buy small quantities of stock at a time and consequently have to pay higher prices than businesses that buy in bulk. An entrepreneur could solve this problem by acting as a part-time buyer for a group of small businesses. In this way, the entrepreneur could obtain bulk prices for them.

Knowledge of these problems enables you, as a prospective entrepreneur, to find the initial idea for a business that is based on the solution of a specific problem.

Page 50 illustrates a technique for generating business ideas formulated by the Scottish Enterprise Foundation in Good Ideas Don't Come Out of the Blue – You Have to Work at Them (1990). This example uses the general problem of traffic jams to illustrate the technique.

Example

Suppose we regard cyclists as a group — those who ride bicycles for recreation. Write down the group's needs as you answer the questions on the next page.
You can use the answers to develop new business ideas.

↪

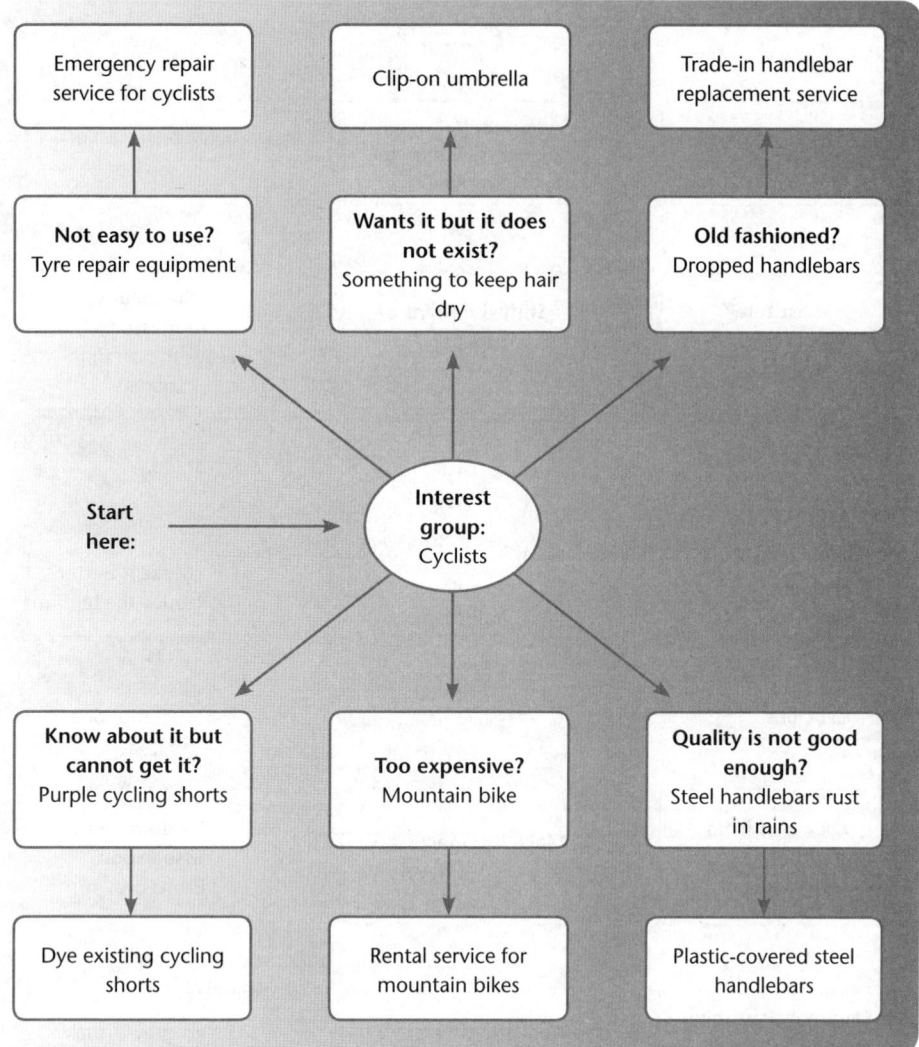

Adapted from *Good Ideas Don't Come Out of the Blue – You Have to Work at Them* (1990)

Example

Cycles, train, bus, taxi

Videos on traffic lights
Banners with useful
information

Traffic queue minder
service

Substitute?
Use another mode of
transport

**Shift the point of
focus?**
Entertain the driver

**Ridiculous
suggestions?**
Leave the car in the
queue

**Start
here:**

**Reduce the
problem?**
Fewer cars

Problem:
Traffic jams

Make it better?
Reduce the tension

Lift clubs

Car phone

**Look at it from
another angle**
Residents

Make it unnecessary?
Do not travel

***Random word
association?**
Plants grown

Earn money washing
cars while you wait in
peak hours

Work and shop close to
home

Roads grow – make
more lanes available

* Use a dictionary or the Yellow Pages and choose any word. Let your mind roam from that word to a solution for the problem.

Adapted from *Good Ideas Don't Come Out of the Blue – You Have to Work at Them* (1990)

3.3.4 The generation of ideas from everyday activities

You can identify many business ideas merely by being aware of the activities that we perform every day. Use the following methods to identify ideas from everyday activities:

- **Use print or electronic media:** Think of the products that are advertised on television, in magazines and in newspapers. Ask yourself whether they can be improved or distributed or marketed in a different way.
- **Look in other places:** You can come up with business ideas by looking in unlikely places. Use the following questions to help:
  - What ideas can you get at an airport, a movie theatre or a church?
  - What ideas can you bring back from a sports meeting, a fun fair or a doctor's consulting room?
- **Explore your surroundings:** Explore a part of your city or town that you have not seen before. What do you notice?
- **Observe other cultures:** Take note of the novelties and different ways of doing things at places where you go on holiday.
- **Talk to other people:** Have conversations with your family, friends, colleagues and businesspeople and find out if they have come across possible business ideas. The problem of obtaining holiday accommodation at short notice could, for example, lead to an enterprise that specialises in finding and allocating unused and cancelled holiday accommodation.
- **At work:** Ask yourself if the products and services at your place of work could be improved upon.
- **Go shopping:** Examine some of the products on your next visit to the shops. Remember that no product or service is perfect. By asking questions about the products, new ideas can emerge. Here are some questions to ask yourself:
  - What problems are there with this product?
  - How can the product be improved in any way?
  - Is there a better way for the product to be packaged?
  - Can any new product be added to the present range of products?
  - Can the product be aimed at another market?

Example

The child-proof lid, which is used on medicine bottles to prevent children opening the bottle, was probably developed after someone thought about the dangers of medicine bottles. Another business idea resulting from everyday activities is renting out evening gowns.

- **Changes in your immediate area:** By noting changes or important events that take place around you, you can identify new business ideas.

Example

If a South African sports team participate in a world cup event, such as the Soccer World cup presented in South African in 2010, this creates an opportunity for an entrepreneur to sell traditionally made or representative items or memorabilia to supporters.

3.3.5 The generation of ideas from other sources

Apart from taking note of everyday activities, you can also find ideas by consulting other reference sources. The following are some examples:

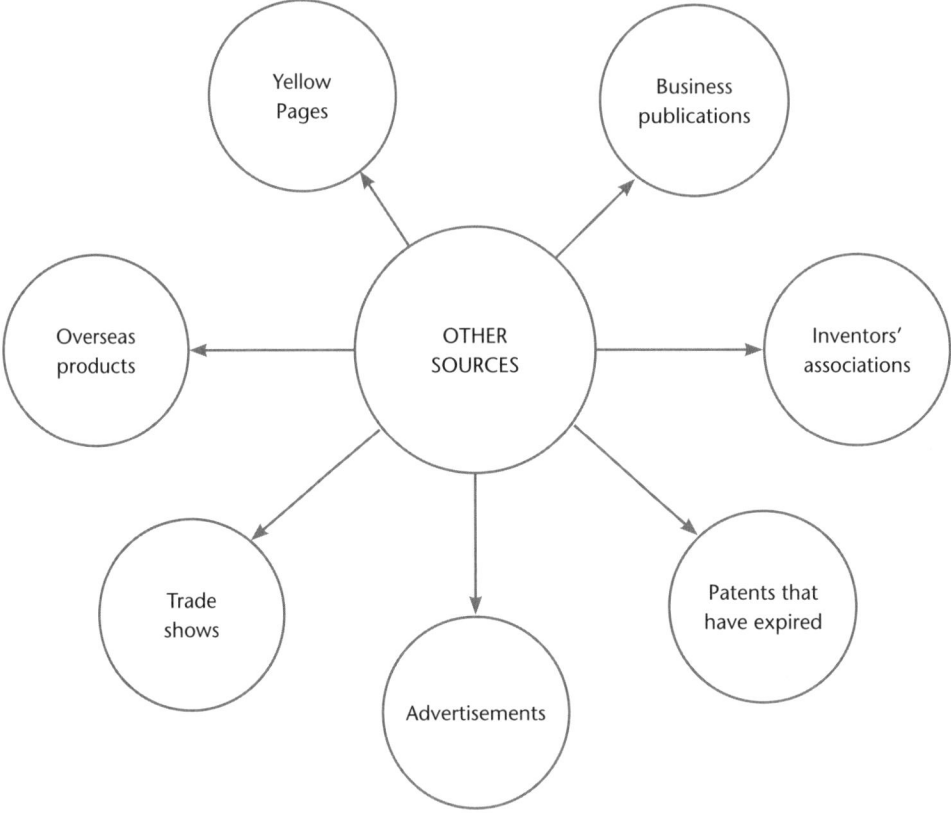

Figure 3.3: A method of generating ideas from other sources

- **The Yellow Pages:** The Yellow Pages lists almost all products and/or services that a business can provide. (It is better to use the Yellow Pages of a large city, as this would contain more information.) By reading the reference index at the end of the Yellow Pages, you can discover a variety of products and/or services in a short space of time. The adverts in the Yellow Pages can provide more information on specific products and/or services.
- **Consult business publications:** Magazines such as *Wealth Wise* and *SA Franchise Warehouse* can be valuable sources of ideas. The *Entrepreneur Magazine South Africa* carries up-to-date success stories on successful entrepreneurs in South Africa.
- **Contact an inventors' association:** This can be a rich source of ideas. For example, you might be able to collaborate with an inventor to produce and market his or her invention. Two associations that might be useful to contact are the Institute of Inventors and the SA Inventors & Designers Society.
- **Examine patents that have expired:** Patents that have expired are public property. There can be various reasons why a patent has not been exploited, and it may now be ready for the market. These reasons could include:

- ○ Bigger markets for the product have arisen in the interim.
- ○ The product can now be used with other products that were previously unavailable.
- ○ The product can be manufactured using new technology, which now makes it technically feasible and commercially viable.
- ○ New use for the product has arisen.
- ○ An example of an expired patent is antibiotics and pills to alleviate muscular injuries. Lennon Medicines sell a product called Panamor that is comparable to the well-known product Voltaren. Panamor originated on the expiry of a patent on the original product.

- **Investigate advertisements for business opportunities:** Newspapers and magazines often carry advertisements for business opportunities. Although many of these must be investigated with caution, there are real opportunities and these can serve as sources of new business ideas. Note, for example, how many franchising opportunities are advertised in the newspapers.
- **Visit trade shows:** Trade shows are a good source of ideas. You also get the opportunity to see the physical product and to talk to the exhibitors about the potential market, product features, new technology and even the possibility of doing business together. Examples are the annual Design Indaba in Cape Town and the Grand Designs show in Johannesburg.
- **Examine overseas products:** Products that are not yet available in South Africa are often imported, imitated or adapted for the South African market. Chicken Licken is an example of a South African business that originated from a business idea obtained abroad and which has been developed into the biggest fried chicken franchised brand outside the United States.

3.4   The development and evaluation of business ideas

In the previous section you were encouraged not to limit your creativity but to think about all possible business ideas. Most of these ideas will not work, however. The initial sifting of ideas is performed by relying on your personal judgement and 'gut feeling'.

Only one of your ideas can be chosen and converted into a business on its own or in combination with one or more of the other ideas on your list. To choose the correct business idea, you must evaluate each idea on your list.

Although there are examples of entrepreneurs who have converted an idea into a successful business opportunity merely on the strength of their intuition, this is not the best way. (Henry Ford, the creator of the Model T Ford, is an example of someone who followed his intuition and made millions from it.)

Business ideas can be evaluated chiefly by means of two methods, namely a feasibility study and a viability study.

Definition

A **feasibility study** is a general examination of the potential of the idea to be converted into a business enterprise. This study focuses largely on the ability of the entrepreneur to convert the idea into a business enterprise.

A **viability study** is an in-depth investigation into profitability of the idea to be converted into a business enterprise.

Before you can start evaluating your idea, you must first be clear about what each of these ideas means. In particular, two things must be clear:

1. what the chief activities of the business will be
2. who the customers will be.

The activities of the business will consist of two or more of the following:

1. the manufacture of a product
2. the provision of a service
3. the sale of other people's products and/or services.

Your customers will consist of:

* individuals and/or
* organisations.

These concepts can be illustrated by means of the following 'bow-tie' diagram.

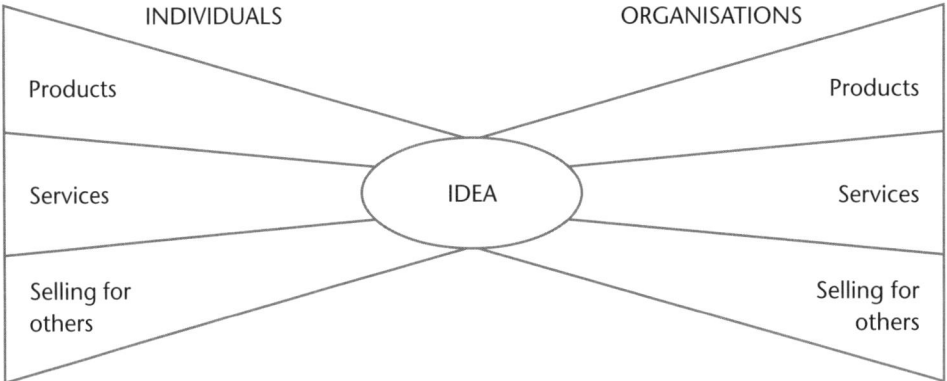

Figure 3.4: Bow-tie diagram
Adapted from *Good Ideas Don't Come Out of the Blue – You Have to Work at Them* (1990)

The bow-tie diagram provides six options for your business, namely:

1. the manufacture of products for individuals
2. the provision of services for individuals
3. the sale of other people's products and/or services to individuals
4. the manufacture of products for organisations
5. the provision of services for organisations
6. the sale of other people's products and/or services to organisations.

3.4.1   The development of your business ideas

The bow-tie diagram can also be used to develop your business idea in terms of:

* the essence of the idea
* the possible combination of ideas
* the possibility of taking a new direction with the idea.

Suppose we take the idea 'to bake cakes'. In the following example you can see all the ideas that might emerge from this one idea.

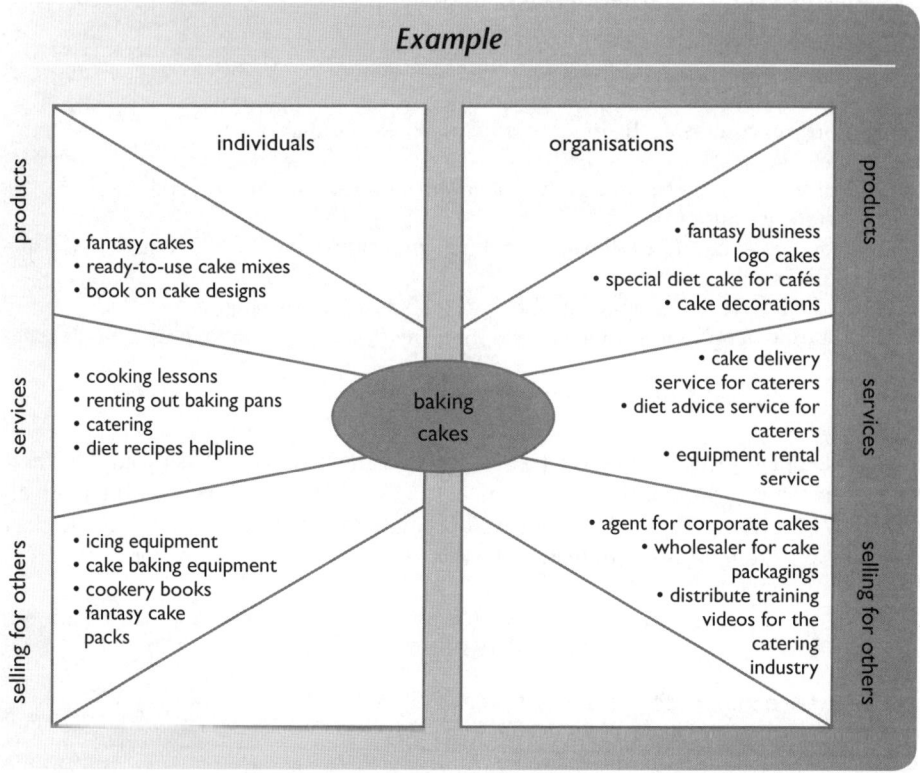

Example

individuals | organisations

products

- fantasy cakes
- ready-to-use cake mixes
- book on cake designs

- fantasy business logo cakes
- special diet cake for cafés
- cake decorations

baking cakes

services

- cooking lessons
- renting out baking pans
- catering
- diet recipes helpline

- cake delivery service for caterers
- diet advice service for caterers
- equipment rental service

selling for others

- icing equipment
- cake baking equipment
- cookery books
- fantasy cake packs

- agent for corporate cakes
- wholesaler for cake packagings
- distribute training videos for the catering industry

Adapted from *Good Ideas Don't Come Out of the Blue – You Have to Work at Them* (1990)

From the above exercise you can see that we can develop the idea 'to bake cakes' further. Here are some examples:

- baking decorative cakes (the essence of the idea)
- making cakes and making and selling cake decorations to bakeries (the combination of ideas)
- producing training DVDs for the catering industry (taking a new direction with the idea).

3.4.2 The feasibility of your business ideas

To determine whether your business idea is feasible, you must be able to answer the following four questions satisfactorily:

1. Do you want to do what the idea suggests?
2. Is there a market for your idea?
3. Can you meet the needs of your customers?
4. Can you advertise the idea to your customers?

To determine the feasibility of your business idea, answer the following questions by filling in a tick (✓) or a question mark (?) in the block alongside each question:

Important information

1. Do you want to do what the idea suggests?

- ☐ Is the idea really something that you want to pursue?
- ☐ Do you want to do business with the types of people who will be your customers?
- ☐ Do you have the health, energy and personality to pursue your idea?
- ☐ Can you cope with the long hours, few—if any—holidays etc associated with this idea?
- ☐ Will you sacrifice the things that are important to you in order to make a successful enterprise out of this idea?
- ☐ Does your family understand the full implications of your decision to start a business?
- ☐ Do you have the support of your family and are they willing to help?
- ☐ Is this idea more important to you than any other idea that you have identified?

Adapted from *Good Ideas Don't Come Out of the Blue – You Have to Work at Them* (1990)

If you filled in any question marks (?) in the blocks above, you must ask yourself whether you really want to pursue this specific idea. In other words, have you got the motivation to achieve success with it? Think of ways to change the question marks (?) into ticks (✓) and how, for example, you can justify the ticks (✓) to your bank manager.

Important information

2. Is there a market for your idea?

- ☐ Do you know who your customers will be?
- ☐ Will they pay you for your product and/or service?
- ☐ Do you think there are many customers for your idea? How many (more or less)?
- ☐ Will people prefer your product and/or service to those of your competitors?
- ☐ Do you think you will gain more customers in the future?
- ☐ What are three advantages you have over your competitors?
- ☐ Can you prevent other people from copying your idea?

Adapted from *Good Ideas Don't Come Out of the Blue – You Have to Work at Them* (1990)

If you filled in any question marks (?) in the blocks above, you must ask yourself whether you have a market for this specific idea. Think of ways to change the question marks (?) into ticks (✓) and how, for example, you can justify the ticks (✓) to someone like your bank manager.

Important information

3. Can you meet the needs of your customers?

- ☐ Do you have, or can you develop, the skills to manufacture your product and/or to provide your service?

➲

☐ Can you provide the quantity and quality of products or give the level of service that your customers want?

☐ Do you know how much money you can charge for your product or service? How much?

☐ If you need someone to help you provide your product or service, do you know anyone who will be willing to do it?

☐ Do you know more or less how much money you will need to start your business? How much?

☐ Do you know how much money you will need in the first year to run your business? How much?

☐ Do you personally have the money to start and run your business? How much do you still need? Where will you get the rest of the money?

Adapted from *Good Ideas Don't Come Out of the Blue – You Have to Work at Them* (1990)

If you filled in any question marks (?) in the list, you must ask yourself if you can pursue this idea. Think of ways to change the question marks (?) into ticks (✓), and how, for example, you can justify the ticks (✓) to someone like your bank manager.

Important information

4. Can you advertise the idea to your customers?

☐ Do you know how your customer buys this product and/or service?

☐ Is there a special magazine, newspaper or journal that your customers read? What is it?

☐ Do you know of any agents or intermediaries who are currently selling to your customers? Who are they?

☐ Do you know of any businesses or organisations who are currently doing business with your customers? Where are they?

☐ Will these businesses or organisations be prepared to promote your idea?

☐ Can you get the names and addresses of a large number of potential customers? About how many?

☐ Do you already have various customers who have indicated that they will buy from you? How many?

Adapted from *Good Ideas Don't Come Out of the Blue – You Have to Work at Them* (1990)

The question marks (?) in the questionnaire above are not very important. What is important is that there must be many ticks (✓). If you do not have any ticks (✓), or only one or two, you must ask yourself if you should pursue this idea. Think of how you can turn the question marks (?) into ticks (✓), and how, for example, you can justify the ticks (✓) to someone like your bank manager.

How do you feel about your business idea now that you have answered all the above questions? Complete the rating scale (Table 3.1) by circling the number that represents your choice. (Idea obtained from the *Good Ideas Don't Come Out of the Blue – You Have to Work at Them*, 1990.)

Table 3.1 Rating Scale

	Level of conviction			
	Very high	High	Average	Low
Do you want to do what the idea suggests?	4	3	2	1
Is there a market for your idea?	4	3	2	1
Can you meet your customers needs?	4	3	2	1
Can you advertise the idea to your customers?	4	3	2	1

By counting the numbers that you circled, you can make the following deductions from your results:

5 or less	If you definitely feel that it is not for you, you must start the process of identifying ideas from the beginning.
6 to 12	If you are still undecided, you must go back to your list of business ideas and consider other options.
12 and above	Your idea is feasible and must be explored further.

If you have found, by means of the results above, that your business idea is in fact feasible, you can go on to investigate its viability. Since the viability study is very expensive in terms of time and money, it is important that you first do the feasibility study as shown above. The next chapter explains step by step the process to investigate the viability of a business idea.

3.5 Summary

In this chapter we took the first step in setting up a business, namely the identification and development of a business idea.

A business idea does not always have to be innovative, but it must stand out from other competitive products or services in some way. This means that the entrepreneur must be able to act creatively. The creative abilities of prospective entrepreneurs can be improved in various ways, such as thinking unconventionally or viewing a matter from another person's perspective or using one of the various group creativity techniques.

The techniques for generating business ideas that are proposed in this book can be divided into five broad approaches: ideas from the skills, expertise and aptitudes of the entrepreneur; ideas from common needs; ideas from existing problems; ideas from everyday activities; and ideas from other sources. These approaches can take place separately or in combination. You might encounter a problem, for example, in a work situation and develop it further by means of the ideas-from-problems technique.

A business idea must be able to be defined in terms of its business activity and customers before it is evaluated and developed.

By matching the business ideas with questions on how the prospective entrepreneur feels about the specific idea, its feasibility can be determined. Business ideas must also be viable before they can be turned into a business. The viability of business ideas is discussed in the next chapter.

Self-evaluation questions

1. List the three stages of setting up a business.
2. Define creativity.
3. Differentiate between divergent and convergent thinking.
4. Perform an online brain dominance test. What is the result of the test and how does it relate to your inclination for creativity?
5. Suppose you and two friends want to start a business together. Explain two creativity techniques that you can use to help you generate business ideas (use one of the techniques explained in this chapter and one technique that you have researched on your own).
6. Generate business ideas from your skills, expertise or aptitude by using the method proposed in this chapter.
7. Generate business ideas from common needs that people have by using the method proposed in this chapter.
8. Generate business ideas from existing problems by using the method proposed in this chapter.
9. Generate business ideas from everyday activities by using the method proposed in this chapter.
10. Generate business ideas from other sources by using the method proposed in this chapter.
11. Take one of your business ideas generated in Questions 6 to 10 and further develop it by using the proposed bow-tie diagram.
12. Determine the feasibility of one of your business ideas by answering the following four broad questions: Do you want to do what the idea suggests? Is there a market for your idea? Can you meet the needs of your customers? Can you advertise the idea to your customers? (Motivate your answers and final conclusion.)
13. No commonly agreed definition of creativity exists. Discuss different views on creativity.
14. Discuss various uses for creativity techniques.
15. Business ideas can be discovered by accident. Debate the pros of this statement versus the pros of a more structured approach in finding business ideas.
16. Discuss the need for both a feasibility and a viability study in setting up a business.

References and further reading

Jacobs, H & Mwile, N. 2011. 'Koljander: The story of success in a South African entrepreneurial home industry business', *Journal of Arts, Science & Commerce*, 2(2): 86–98.

Richardson, P & Clarke, L. 1990. *Good Ideas Don't Come Out of the Blue - You Have to Work at Them.* The Scottish Enterprise Foundation for the Training Agency. Dunedin: Crown.

Nieman, G & Nieuwenhuizen, C (eds). 2009. *Entrepreneurship: A South African Perspective*, 2nd ed. Pretoria: Van Schaik Publishers.

Rwigema, H, Urban, B & Venter, R. 2008. *Entrepreneurship: Theory in Practice*, 2nd ed. Cape Town: Oxford University Press Southern Africa.

Van Aardt, I, Van Aardt, C, Bezuidenhout, S & Mumba, M. 2008. *Entrepreneurship and New Venture Management*. Cape Town: Oxford University Press Southern Africa.

CHAPTER FOUR

The viability of a business idea

Michael Cant

Learning outcomes

After you have studied this chapter, you should be able to:

- perform a viability study for a proposed business idea by doing the following:
  - establishing whether there is a need for a particular product or service
  - defining the mission and objectives for the business
  - estimating the market size and share of the product or service
  - calculating the income that can be derived from the product or service
  - determining the break-even point for the business
  - understanding the implications of calculating the break-even point
  - determining whether a sustainable profit can be made
  - drawing up a cash budget to determine whether the business can service its financial obligations as they occur.

4.1 Introduction

We are now ready to move on to the planning stage of the business (turn back and look at Figure 3.1 again on page 39). It is important to give adequate attention to this stage as it sets the framework in which your business will operate.

There are usually two phases linked to business planning, namely to establish the viability of the idea and then to draw up a business plan. The first phase, to establish whether a business idea is viable, is known as the viability study. For an idea to be a viable business idea, it must be possible for the entrepreneur to be able to market it and to manage the business at a sustainable profit. Only if the idea is found to be viable do you continue to the second phase, namely drawing up the business plan. The business plan summarises the conclusions drawn from the viability study. It can then be used to make the idea known to other people, and to obtain financing to implement the business idea.

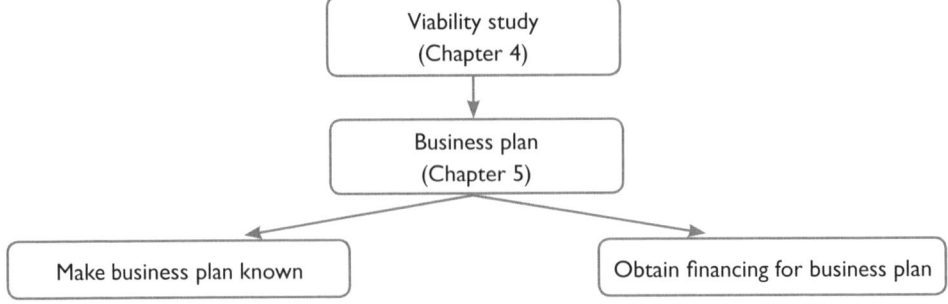

Figure 4.1: The planning stage in establishing a business

An idea is viable if you can market it and manage a business over time at a sustainable profit. This period is usually between two and five years. The viability of an idea must be tested, based on certain assumptions and on research you will have to conduct. The viability study must also make provision for unforeseen circumstances.

Example

What would happen if your business partner decided that he or she did not want to continue doing business with you anymore, or if your bank could no longer support your business? What would you do if the results from the research you conducted did not have the outcome you thought it would have?

4.2 The viability study

Definition

The **viability study** entails estimating the interest in the business and its product or service, the expected sales in units and at a certain price, the expected costs associated with generating the sales, the strengths and weaknesses of the business, and so forth.

Before you can begin work on the viability study, you will have to do some market research and gather various facts and figures to estimate the size of the market. You should not be too optimistic during this phase; it is much better to underestimate the size of the market than to overestimate it.

Definition

These are some of the typical questions you should find answers to:

- Is there a need for my product or service? (**Needs analysis**)
- What type of person (customer) will buy my product or service? (**Customer profile/characteristics**)
- What can realistically be expected to be sold of this product or service based on the estimated market size? (**Market share**)
- How much are customers willing to pay for the product or service? (**Price analysis**)

Based on the information received from the market research, some assumptions can be made. These include the following:

- the estimated number of units that will be sold
- the acceptable price that the market will be prepared to pay for the product or service
- the cash-flow requirements for the business.

It is therefore essential that the entrepreneur do a proper needs analysis of the market as well as identifying the characteristics of customers. The section below explains how to do this.

4.3   The needs analysis and characteristics of customers

As an entrepreneur, the very first thing you should do is find out exactly who your potential customers are, what their needs are and how they make their buying decisions. The key to success is to make sure that the product or service you offer is what the customer wants and not just what you want to sell.

In order to be able to make a decision on the viability of your idea or business, you must have information on the characteristics, needs and purchasing patterns of the customers. Given the intense competition in the market today, reliable information is the key to a successful business.

In Chapter 2 we explained that people buy in order to satisfy a need. However, this concept of buying to satisfy a need is not that clear or straightforward. On the one hand, a need can be very strongly felt but not easily defined but, on the other hand, there can be various options for satisfying that need. There is generally a distinct difference between the physical product that customers buy and the image customers have of the product. When you are about to provide a product or service to the market, you must determine which need that product or service will satisfy.

To do this, you need to be very specific about who your customers are and be able to develop a customer profile. A profile is nothing more that a description of the potential customers. You must be able to determine their distinguishing characteristics and then look for information about their location and numbers.

Example

An example of a customer profile would be:

Age and sex:
Females between the ages of 18 and 25

Social status:
Socially active and health conscious

Income:
Annual income of R100 000 to R150 000

Geographic region:
All major metropolitan areas

The needs of the customer forms the basis of any marketing strategy and therefore it is essential that you know what customers want and to establish if you can meet that need – and make a profit. Therefore it is important that you establish how you can provide the right product or service at the right price at the right time in order to make a profit. If you cannot make a profit within a certain period of time, there is no sense in entering that market.

To establish if there is a need for a product or service, you must define the market in terms of its total size, that is the group or groups of potential customers to whom you will be marketing your business. You should also identify the market where your product/s will be most widely accepted.

Important information

To establish if there is a need for a particular product or service, you can ask these questions to conduct your market research:

1. **List the features of the product or service.** This will help you to focus on each aspect of your product or service and to decide whether it meets the needs of the market. For example, your product may be a new facial cream. The features of the cream may be that it moisturises, has an anti-ageing component, rejuvenates the skin and has a SPF 50⁺.

2. **Determine who the major competitors are and who the industry leaders are, as well as suppliers and other major role-players in this market.** This section is very important as it forces you to examine the industry as a whole, in order to determine its place in the market. You need to look at the size of your competitors and how they compete in the marketplace. If, for example, competition is largely on price, you may want to stay out of the market as customer loyalty will be low in such a market. Not only must you look at direct competition (other cosmetic suppliers and manufacturers) but you also need to look at indirect competition (customers might prefer to spend their money on cosmetic surgery or endermologie and not creams). In a similar way, you should identify and evaluate your suppliers. Suppliers vary; some are reliable and deliver the right product on time at a good price and others do not.

3. **Identify the possible customers and segment of the market.** To do this, you need to define the market in terms of its total size and target market. Each market must be examined carefully in terms of overall size, demand and potential profitability. It is not possible to try and satisfy all segments so it is better to focus on that part that is most likely to buy your product. Determining which market segments are most attractive is called **market segmentation**. Market research will be crucial to obtain this information. Let's say that market research shows that middle-aged females between the ages of 40 and 55 are most likely to buy this facial cream.

4. **Draw up a final list.** This should include:
   o the features of your product or service
   o the needs of the customers that the product or service will meet
   o a profile of your customers
   o the potential number of customers.

Once you have this information, you can determine what kind of business you wish to start. You can then also define your business and determine its objectives.

4.4 The business structure

4.4.1 Types of business structures

There are several options with regard to the structure of your business. The criterion are discussed below:

Table 4.1 Different business structures

Type of ownership	No. of owners
Sole trader/proprietor	1
Partnership	2–20
Close corporation	1–10
Company	1–50

Sole trader or sole proprietor

This is a business structure where there is one owner and registering of the business is not required. For example, Violet would like to start a hair salon in her garage. When a sole trader is formed, there is no differentiation between the assets of the business and the owner. Therefore, everything in Violet's house (ie the hairdryer, the salon chair, her bed and fridge) is under the same form of ownership.

The debt owing to creditors is also not separated between the business and the owner. Therefore, if the business fails to repay a debt, the creditors have the right to seize personal assets. For example, if Violet's hair salon runs out of money to repay her loan from the bank, the creditors have a right to seize everything she owns.

Partnership

In a partnership the partners own the business together. A partnership can be between two to twenty people and is signed as a written agreement either prepared by the partners or by a lawyer. Should it happen that a new partner joins the partnership then a new agreement needs to be compiled. The agreement needs to address the issues such as: profit share and terms of termination.

The same as for a sole trader, there is no differentiation in a partnership between the assets and debts of the owners and the business. The law does not recognise a difference between different partners' assets and debts. For example, if Violet and Lebo's catering business fails to repay its debts, then the creditors could legally pursue their funds by recovering the money from the selling of Violet and Lebo's cars and houses.

Close corporation

A close corporation or CC is registered as a business entity. The group of individuals who own and manage the closed corporation should not be more than ten and they are referred to as members.

Unlike partnerships and sole traders, the assets and debts of a CC are not legally bounded to the members of the business. For example, if Violet and Lebo formed a CC and their business failed to repay its debts, the creditors could only recover the money from the selling of the CC's assets and not the members' personal assets unless they have stood surety in their personal capacity. The registration of a CC can be done with a lawyer or accountant and the business will be given a registration number. From 1 May 2011, however, this form of business structure is not possible anymore.

Company

A company is formed when more than ten people would like to start a business and they prefer to create a separate legal entity. A company consists of shareholders and directors, where shareholders refers to the owners of the business and directors refers to the managers of the business. Shareholders and directors could also be the same people.

Like a CC, a company has a legal entity. Therefore, its debts and assets are seen as separate to those of the shareholders and directors.

4.4.2   Legal considerations

New Companies Act

There are various legal implications when starting a business. A company is governed by the Companies Act and a CC by the Close Corporations Act. There are some recent developments with regard to the new Companies Act which came into effect on 1 May 2011.

From the official implementation of the new Companies Act, no more close corporations will be allowed. The act allows for existing close corporations to convert into a private company should the members decide to do so. From the effective date of the Act, companies will no longer be able to convert into a close corporation.

The following are additional requirements of the new Companies Act:

- **Companies**: The Act makes provision for profit and non-profit companies. Certain private companies are recognised, such as personal liability companies (Inc) and the normal private companies ((Pty) Ltd). In addition, public companies (Ltd) are also recognised. Although existing close corporations are recognised, new ones will not be registered. State-owned companies are also recognised and known by the Non Profit Company (NPC) behind the names.
- **Founding statement**: The memorandum of articles of association no longer applies. It has been replaced by the Memorandum of Incorporation, known as the MOI. In terms of the New Companies Act, a company may exclude or include specific provisions of the New Companies Act in its MOI. This means that depending on the founders/owners they may decide to include or exclude restrictions on aspects such as signing powers, operational issues and so on.
- **Transparency**: Companies will now be more accountable for their actions and greater transparency will be required to protect the public and shareholders (Summary of new companies act, Department of Trade and Industry, 2011).

Consumer Protection Act

The new Consumer Protection Act (CPA) came into effect on 1 April 2011 and will be implemented by the National Consumer Commission (NCC), which has taken over from the department of Trade and Industry's Office of Consumer Protection (OCP) (Department of Trade and Industry, 2011).

The CPA will protect the general public by allowing the consumers to:

- cancel or renew a fixed-term agreement
- cancel direct marketing contracts within the cooling-off period
- stop the usage of their data for direct marketing purposes
- choose or examine goods, even after purchase and delivery
- return goods and seek redress for unsatisfactory services
- retain and not pay for unsolicited goods or services and
- cancel advance reservations.

Sections 20 and 56 of the CPA emphasise the right to choose, as well as the right to fair value and good quality, which provide consumers with redress on unsatisfactory goods and services. The envisaged outcome of the campaign is to ensure that consumers are able to:

- make well-informed buying decisions
- access a wide range of products and services, based on honest and fair marketing and selling practices
- have access to efficient and effective redress and
- know and understand their rights and responsibilities.

4.4.3   A practical checklist when starting a business

The following checklist is a general description of the steps that a start-up company may follow. It is taken from the website of the Companies and Intellectual Companies Registration Office (CIPRO).

1. Decide on the type of business entity that you wish to form – a public or private company.
2. Choose your enterprise's name and think about at least two alternative names.
3. Draw up your business plan.
4. Await your enterprise registration number from Companies and Intellectual Property Commission (CIPC).
5. After receiving your enterprise number, apply for your VAT (Value Added Tax) number, income tax number, PAYE (Pay as you earn), SDL (Skills Development Levy) and UIF (Unemployment Insurance Fund) numbers from the South African Revenue Service (SARS).
6. Register your logo as a trademark with CIPC.
7. Ensure that all of the enterprise's intellectual property is copyrighted.
8. If you have a unique product that you would like to patent, register this as a patent with CIPC. Registering for copyright, patents, trademarks and designs is not compulsory for every enterprise.

It must be noted that from 1 May 2011 CIPRO (Companies and Intellectual Properties Registration Office) ceased to exist and the new Companies Act came into effect. This led to the birth of CIPC (Companies and Intellectual Property Commission), which now regulates all areas related to intellectual property. The CIPC is a merger of the Companies and Intellectual Property Registration Office (CIPRO) and the Office of the Company and Intellectual Property Enforcement. This also came into effect on 1 May 2011. Responsibilities of the CIPC will include registering companies, promoting awareness of company and intellectual property law and monitoring compliance of financial reporting standards (http://www.fin24.com/Economy/Body-to-replace-Cipro-launched-20110418). Visit www.cipc.co.za for more details on CIPC.

4.5   The mission statement and objectives of the business

In Chapter 2, the mission statement and objectives of the business were broadly described as 'what you want to achieve and how you will achieve it'. In this section we will look at these in more detail. By this stage, you probably know what type of business you would like to run. It is therefore possible to move on to defining the mission statement and objectives. This is an important task and deserves some time and thought.

It is usual to define a business according to the product or service that you wish to sell, as well as by the customer profile. The definition must not be too narrow or too broad. If it is too narrow, it might exclude possible opportunities, but a definition that is too general can cause a lack of focus. The following questions will help you define your business:

- Who are the customers of the business?
- Which customer needs will the business satisfy?
- How will the business satisfy these needs?

By following the steps outlined on page 66, you have already collected the information to answer these questions. You can now proceed to defining the mission statement.

4.5.1 Mission statement

A business is defined by its mission statement. Only a clear definition of the mission and purpose of the business makes it possible for clear and realistic objectives. Most companies have their mission statement on their website. For example, search for the Vodacom site; their mission statement clearly describes what they want to achieve.

Definition

A **mission statement** defines the fundamental and unique purpose of a business and identifies its products or services, as well as its customers. The mission of a business is defined by customer's satisfaction with its products and services.

Questions that need to be answered when formulating the mission statement are as follows:

- Who are the customers?
- Why do they buy?
- What do they buy?
- How do they buy?
- Where are they located?
- How can the customers be reached?
- What, in the opinion of the customer, is value for money?

Example

Here is an example of a software developer's mission statement:

'To deliver the best solutions to software problems through proper understanding of the problems, insight, above-average effort and high quality service.'

After you have set the mission statement, you can now formulate objectives for your business. The objectives must be measurable, realistic, clear, attainable and within a set time frame.

> ## Definition
>
> An **objective** is something the business wants to achieve over a set period of time.

> ## Example
>
> An example of an **objective** could be to show a 15% return on capital within the first two years of the business's existence.

Objectives are necessary so that you have something against which to measure progress. They are usually adjusted over time, based on changes that take place in the industry and environment.

Defining your mission statement and objectives clarifies what your business is all about. It will also help you calculate your market share, so that you can work out if your product or service can be marketed profitably. You must make realistic predictions. Whatever you do, do not be too optimistic; it does not help to mislead yourself. If you are too optimistic, it could lead to failure.

4.6   Calculating the expected market share

The next step in the planning process is to determine the expected market share for your product or service. It is important to calculate this as accurately as possible, because this share will be used as a basis to estimate the potential income of your business. Again, we must stress that you should not overestimate the potential market as this will give you a false sense of what your income could be.

To calculate the expected market share you need to:

- estimate the total potential market for your product or service
- estimate what portion of the market is occupied by your competitors
- estimate what portion you can expect to sell to (this is know as your target market).

A method for calculating these figures follows to help you calculate your expected market share.

4.6.1   Calculating the potential market

It is not easy to estimate a potential market. Most entrepreneurs work with unquantified information and must make many assumptions. However, when you identified the need for your product, you collected much of the information needed to segment your market.

When trying to establish the potential market, you should begin by dividing it into various market segments.

> ## Example
>
> A restaurant in Johannesburg cannot cater for all the needs and tastes in the food market. The entrepreneur must therefore select a specific segment of the total market to service. For instance, the entrepreneur must decide whether to sell Italian or Mexican food. The segment that is chosen is then called the **target market** and consists of customers with similar needs and tastes.

Establishing your target market consists of three steps:

- market segmentation
- evaluation and the target-market decision
- market positioning.

1. Market segmentation

Market segmentation is the process whereby the total market is identified and divided into subgroups or segments with similar needs. The market can be sub-divided into the following segments:

- **Demographic segmentation:** Demographic features such as age, gender and race are useful for describing customers with similar needs.

Example

My target market can be males in the age group 25 to 35, of Indian decent and who fall in the higher income group.

- **Geographical segmentation:** It is not always possible to service everybody who might be a potential customer and therefore you may decide, for example, to focus only on Cape Town and Hermanus initially.
- **Psychographic segmentation:** Customers can be grouped on the basis of their personality or lifestyle, for instance those who enjoy the outdoors and like 4X4 driving.
- **Behaviouristic segmentation:** Some people may prefer seafood to Italian food, some prefer quiet, romantic settings, while others enjoy lively music and dancing while they eat. Some only eat out on special occasions and others eat out at least once a week. You should note that customer behaviour differs.

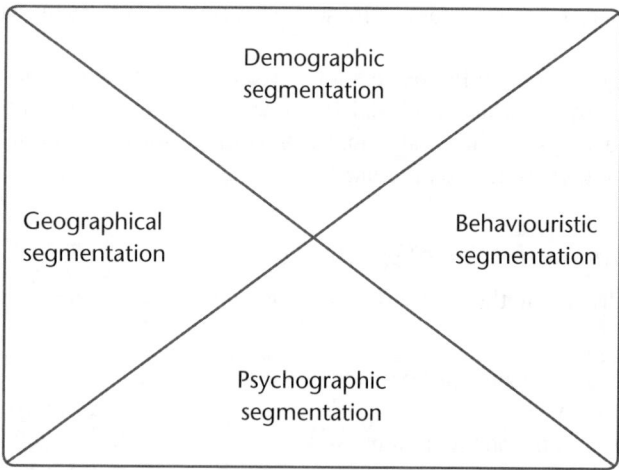

Figure 4.2: Market segmentation

Important information

Because there are various ways to segment the market, you must select appropriate criteria for your product or service. This table gives some examples.

Table 4.2 Criteria for Segmentation

Product or service	Characteristics	Segmentation
Safety doors	Cares for the family, needs protection whilst on holiday.	Psychographic
Sports goods	Used for exercise and entertainment.	Demographic and psychographic
Restaurants	Visited for celebrations and entertainment.	Behaviouristic

2. Evaluation and the target-market decision

After you have grouped the total market into segments, you must select one segment as your target market and focus your marketing campaigns on that specific segment. The choice of your segment should be governed by such things as accessibility (for advertising purposes) and size (to generate enough profit).

If most customers (size) in an area prefer Indian food to Chinese food, and there is no restaurant in the area, it is logical to cater for Indian food (accessibility) as this will generate more sales and greater profit.

3. Market positioning

If you choose more than one segment as your target market, you must design a different marketing campaign for each segment. For example, one market segment prefers Indian food and the other segment prefers Chinese food; advertising to each of these segments will differ.

In summary, it is usually impossible for any one entrepreneur to focus on the total market. It is usually preferable and realistic to focus on one segment only. We call this the target-market decision. Successful entrepreneurs go for a large share in one segment, rather than a small share in the total market.

4.6.2 Calculating the size of the market

Here is the traditional method for estimating the market size of your target market:

Number of customer units	(1)
Average annual gross income per unit	(2)
Total income for area	(1 x 2 = 3)
Percentage (%) of income spent on item	(4)
Potential rand value for item	(3 x 4 = 5)
Realistic percentage (%) of entrepreneur's market share	(6)
Rand value of entrepreneur's market share	(5 x 6 = 7)

Example

John Student intends selling cigarettes and soft drinks on a part-time basis at college. There are 880 students and the average annual income per student is R1 000. On average the students spend 20% of their income on cigarettes and soft drinks. John is convinced that he will attract 5% of the market share, as there is already a cafeteria at the college and also other competitors where the students live and on their way to college. What is the potential rand value of this market?

Answer

1.	Number of customer units	880
2.	Average annual gross income	R1 000
3.	Total income of students	R880 000
4.	Percentage spent on items	20%
5.	Potential rand value of market	R176 000
6.	Realistic percentage of market share	5%
7.	Rand value of John's market share	R8 800

The rand value of John's sales amounts to R8 800 a year. This is not his profit, but his turnover. This rough estimate gives the entrepreneur an idea of the market potential. **Be careful not to be over-optimistic of your potential market share.**

If John is happy with his rand value, he can continue with his business plans. If he is unhappy with the market share, he should research another business idea.

Important information

To retain this market share or even increase it, the entrepreneur should market products in such a way as to attract customers from other competitors.

Example

How do we determine the number of units, average income, percentage spent on items, etc? This information can be found in reports in newspapers, from government departments, municipalities and research bureaus of universities.

4.6.3   Calculating the expected market share

There may be times when a business cannot satisfy the demand for a product or service because its capacity restricts the number of products that it can produce. At other times, the economy may be in decline, and customers may not be able to satisfy their need for the product, because they do not have the necessary money or credit to buy it. Because the economy and external environment changes, you should determine what your expected market share would be under these varying circumstances.

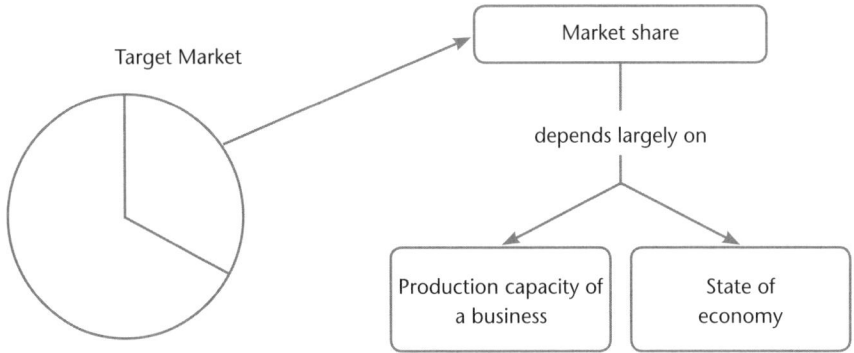

> ### Definition
>
> The **expected market share** is that part of the target market that a business will be able to serve on the basis of its production capacity and the state of the economy.

Figure 4.3: Estimating the expected market share

Source: Nieuwenhuizen C et al, *Basics of Entrepreneurship* 2nd ed (2004)

It is not easy to estimate the expected market share but it is important to do this as accurately as possible in order to calculate a realistic potential income. In order to be realistic and to reduce risk, you should calculate three scenarios:

* a very prosperous one
* a very conservative one and
* a most likely one.

The average of the three scenarios could be taken as the one to work from. Remember that if you 'manipulate' or inflate the figures, you will only be fooling yourself!

You should then calculate the profit for each scenario and judge from that whether it is worth going ahead with the business idea. (See page 77 for an explanation of how to calculate your profit.) This kind of calculation is imperative if you intend to obtain financing from a source such as a bank.

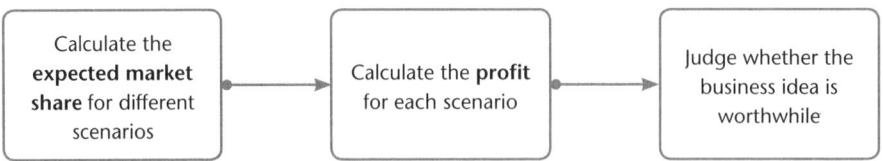

Figure 4.4: Calculating whether the business idea is worthwhile

Source: Nieuwenhuizen C et al, *Basics of Entrepreneurship* 2nd ed (2004)

4.7 Calculating the income

To calculate the potential income for your business, you have to work out the selling price of your product or service. To do this, you must establish exactly what costs will be incurred to manufacture and sell the product. You must first know what the total cost per unit (cost price) will be before you can calculate the selling price (see Section 4.7.1 below).

The selling price must at least cover all the costs. If the costs are not covered, the business will show a loss from the start and will not survive.

After the costs per unit have been established, the next step in calculating the selling price is to add a percentage profit (mark-up) to the cost price (cost price + profit = selling price).

If you add a mark-up of 40% and the cost price of the product is R10, the product will sell at 140/100 x R10 = R14,00.

To calculate the selling price by adding a mark-up to the cost price, you must add the percentage mark-up to 100 and then divide it by 100. You then multiply the answer by the cost price of the product.

Example

If you have a 40% mark-up and the cost price of the product is R10, the selling price will be:

40 + 100 = 140

140/100

= 1,40

1,40 x 10 = R14,00 (selling price)

Put differently, the selling price would be R10 plus R4 = R14,00
If you have a 60% mark-up and the cost price of the product is R20, the selling price will be:

60 + 100 = 160

160/100

= 1,6

1,6 x 20 = R32 (selling price)

When deciding what the mark-up and selling price should be, you need to look at what the market price is (what your competitors are charging for the same product). If your market analysis has shown that the market is price sensitive, you must charge a price that is competitive. If the market is not price sensitive, then you may get away with charging a higher price if the product can be differentiated.

4.7.1   Calculating the cost price of the product

When calculating the cost price it is important to classify the costs as either:

*   variable and fixed costs or
*   direct and indirect costs.

Variable and fixed costs

Variable costs are costs that are fixed per unit, but variable in total. This means that the costs rises in relation to the number of units manufactured (see the graph in Figure 4.5).

For example, if the raw materials in a product cost R1, and 10 products are manufactured, the total variable cost is R10. If 20 products are manufactured, the total variable cost is R20, but it is still R1 for one product.

We can show variable costs on a graph as follows:

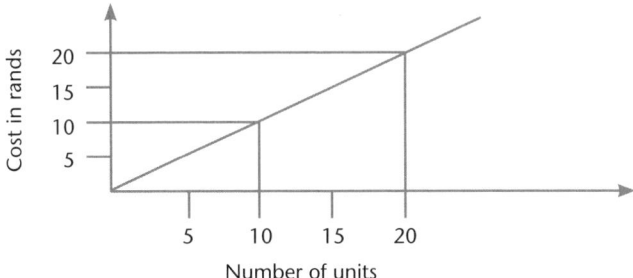

Figure 4.5: Variable costs

Fixed costs are the costs that are fixed in total, but variable per unit. Look at the following graph. The rent on a factory is R100 (point A). This means that if you make 10 units of your product, each one costs R10 to make. If 20 products are manufactured, the total fixed cost is still R100 (point B), but each unit costs R5 to make.

We can show fixed costs on a graph as follows:

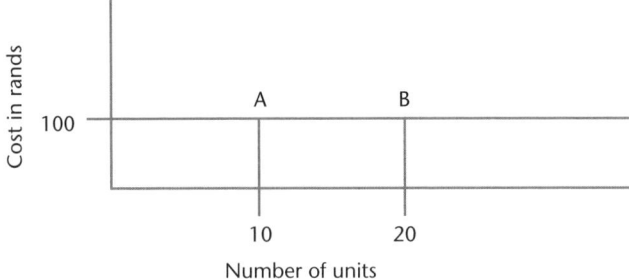

Figure 4.6: Fixed costs

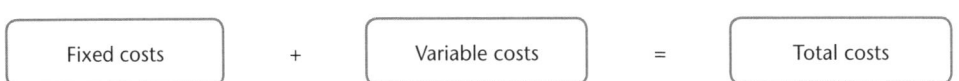

Figure 4.7: Calculating total costs

Direct and indirect costs

Direct costs are costs that can be allocated directly to the manufacture of the product. Examples of direct costs are the raw materials used for the manufacture of a product, and wages of labourers who are directly involved in manufacturing the product.

Indirect costs (also called overheads) are costs that cannot be allocated directly to a product. Examples of these are rent on the factory, electricity, water, depreciation and indirect wages (like the salary of the owner).

Calculating the total costs per unit of the product

There are various ways of calculating the cost of a product in a business, depending on the type of business. These are discussed on the next page:

Calculating the total costs per unit of a product for a manufacturing business

The total costs of a product in a manufacturing business consists of manufacturing costs plus commercial overhead costs.

- **Manufacturing costs:** These consist of direct labour costs (the wages of the factory workers), direct material costs (the costs of raw materials) and manufacturing overhead costs (indirect costs).

Figure 4.8: Calculating manufacturing costs

- **Commercial overhead costs:** These consist of administrative overheads and marketing overheads. The administrative overhead costs are all costs related to the administration of the business functions, such as human resources, finance and management. Marketing costs are all the costs incurred in marketing the product, such as advertising.

Figure 4.9: Calculating commercial overheads

Follow these steps to calculate the total costs of one unit of a product:

- Calculate the direct costs of the materials that are used to manufacture one unit of a product.
- Calculate the direct labour costs needed to manufacture one unit of a product.
- Calculate the indirect costs per unit of the product. (Add the manufacturing overheads, marketing overheads and administrative overheads together and divide this total by the number of products that were manufactured in the same period the costs were incurred; for example, one month.)
- Add the costs together to get the total costs per unit.

Direct costs of materials + Direct labour costs + Indirect costs = Total costs

Figure 4.10: Costs per unit for a manufacturing business

Calculating the total costs per hour for a service business

In a service business, the product that is for sale is knowledge and skill. An example of this would be a business that repairs computer equipment. In this kind of business, an hourly rate for labour must be calculated.

Follow these steps to calculate the total costs of one unit of 'product':

- **Calculate the number of business hours per month:** (This is the number of hours during which the business operates). For example, daily from 8:00 to 17:00 (in other words, 9 hours a day):

6 days a week x 9 hours = 54 hours a week x 52 weeks = 2 808 hours a year ÷ 12 months = 234 hours a month.

- **Calculate the cost per hour:** To do this, calculate the total expenses for a month, for example rent on the building, salaries and rental on office equipment. Suppose it is R10 000 a month. Divide the total costs by the number of working hours per month: R10 000 ÷ 234 hours = R42,73 an hour. This means that you cannot charge less than R42,73 an hour for your services.

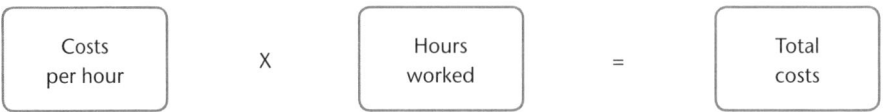

Figure 4.11: Total costs of a product for a service business

Calculating the total costs per product for a commercial business

A commercial business does not manufacture products. It buys finished products and then sells them again at a higher price. The total costs for a product in a commercial business are made up of the purchasing costs of the product to be sold (the cost of sales) plus the commercial overhead costs.

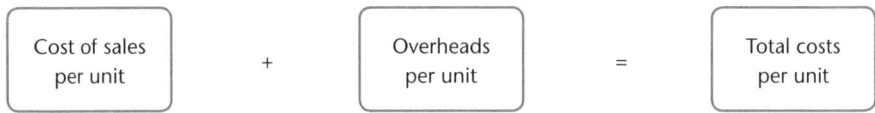

Figure 4.12: Total costs of a product for a commercial business

4.7.2 Calculating the selling price

The price you can charge for your product or service is directly influenced by the price that your competitors charge for the same kind of product or service. If your product or service is much more expensive than that of your competitors, you will lose customers. Your product or service can only be more expensive than that of your competitors if you offer more benefits than your competitors – this means that the market must perceive that they are getting more value for money.

To determine what you can charge for your product, make a list of your products and then establish what your competitors charge for similar products. Next list the competitors' strengths and weaknesses alongside your business's strengths and weaknesses, and compare the two lists in Table 4.3.

Table 4.3 Comparison of strengths and weaknesses

Your own business	Competitor's business
List of products and prices	List of products and prices
1. .... R.............	1. .... R.............
2. .... R.............	2. .... R.............
3. .... R.............	3. .... R.............

You can now establish what the highest and lowest prices are and also what price range (the prices charged for the product or service in general) apply to the product or service. If a business has exceptional strengths, this can justify higher prices. The opposite is also true: if the business has many weaknesses it will be obliged to charge lower prices than its competitors.

After you have made the comparison, you can decide what you can charge for your product or service. Remember that you may never charge less than the total cost of a product or service unless such a product is used as a loss leader to bring customers into the store.

Once the selling price has been established, the potential income and net profit from the sale of the product can be calculated.

4.8   Calculating the expected net profit

After establishing the costs and mark-up for your product, you are now ready to test the viability of the business. To be viable, the business idea must be profitable. To establish whether the business is going to be profitable, the expected unit sales must be multiplied by the expected selling price to arrive at the turnover. From this figure, deduct the expected costs. The difference will be the profit. If the income exceeds the expenses, you will be making a profit. If, on the other hand, your expenses exceed your income, you will be making a loss.

The net profit is calculated by drawing up a pro forma income statement.

Definition

A **pro forma** Income statement is one that is drawn up using estimated figures.

You can calculate the net profit using the figures you arrived at for the various scenarios discussed under Section 4.6.3.

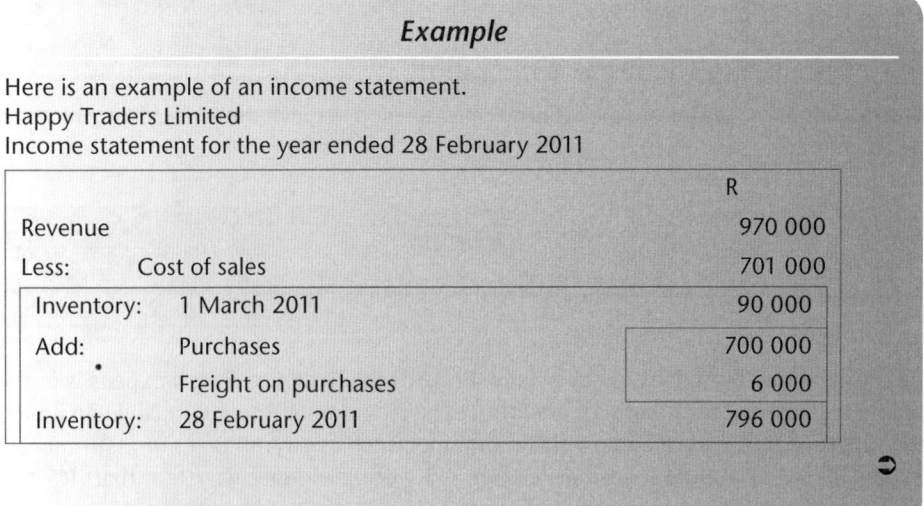

Example

Here is an example of an income statement.
Happy Traders Limited
Income statement for the year ended 28 February 2011

		R
Revenue		970 000
Less:	Cost of sales	701 000
Inventory:	1 March 2011	90 000
Add:	Purchases	700 000
	Freight on purchases	6 000
Inventory:	28 February 2011	796 000

Gross profit (970 000–701 000)	269 000
Add: Discount received	4 000
Total	273 000
Less: Selling, administrative and general expenses	178 450
Freight on sales	4 000
Discount allowed	3 000
Commission to sales personnel	9 000
Salaries and wages	95 450
Stationery and postage	3 000
Bad debts	2 500
Insurance	6 000
Sundry expenses	16 000
Auditor's remuneration	6 500
Director's remuneration	15 000
Loss on sale of equipment	2 000
Depreciation	16 000
Profit from operations (273 000 – 178 450)	94 550
Investment income	5 000
Listed investments	2 000
Unlisted investments	3 000
Less: Finance costs	(14 300)
Interest on bank overdraft	(2 000)
Interest on mortgage loan	(4 800)
Interest on debentures	(7 500)
Profit before tax	83 450
Income tax (29%)	24 200,50
Net profit for the year	59 249,50

4.9   Calculating the break-even point

For any business, the gross sales volume level needed to reach the break-even point must be calculated.

Definition

Break-even is the volume where all fixed expenses are covered.

Begin the break-even analysis by establishing all the fixed (overhead) expenses of your business. Since most of these are monthly expenses, do not forget to include an amount for expenses that are paid quarterly or annually, such as payroll taxes or insurance. For example, if your annual insurance charge is R9 000, use one twelfth of that (R750) as part of your monthly budget. With the semi-variable expenses, such as phone charges, travel and marketing, use a figure that you expect to spend each and every month.

Example

For the purpose of a model break-even calculation, let us assume that the fixed expenses for Happy Traders are as follows:

Administrative salaries	R1 500
Rent	R800
Utilities	R300
Insurance	R150
Taxes	R210
Telephone	R240
Car expense	R400
Supplies	R100
Sales and marketing	R300
Interest	R100
Miscellaneous	R400
Total	R4 500

These are the expenses that must be covered by your gross profit. Assuming that the gross profit margin is 30%, what sales volume must you achieve to cover these expenses? The answer in this case is R15 000; 30% of that amount is R4 500, which is your target figure.

The two critical numbers in these calculations are the total fixed expenses and the percentage of gross profit margin. If your fixed expenses are R10 000 and your gross profit margin is 25%, your break-even figure must be R40 000.

Along the way, expenses tend to creep into both the direct and indirect categories. Therefore it is important to look at your profit and loss statement every six months or so and recalculate your break-even target number.

4.9.1   Ways to lower the break-even volume

There are mainly three ways to lower your break-even volume; only two of them involve cost controls (which should always be your goal!).

1. **Lower direct costs, which will raise the gross margin:** Be more diligent about purchasing material, controlling inventory or increasing the productivity of your labour by more cost-effective scheduling or adding more efficient technology.
2. **Exercise cost controls on your fixed expenses:** Be careful when cutting expenses that you do so with an overall plan in mind. You can cut too deeply as well as too little and cause distress among workers, or you may pull back marketing efforts at the wrong time, which will give out the wrong signal.
3. **Raise prices!** Most entrepreneurs are reluctant to raise prices because they think that business will fall off. More often than not that does not happen unless you are in a very price-sensitive market and, if you are, you have probably already become volume driven.

If you are in the typical niche-type small business, you can raise your prices 4–5% without your customers noticing. The effect is startling.

Example

Look at the difference in the following example:

Volume	R15 000	
Direct cost	R10 500	(70%)
Gross profit	R4 500	

Raising the price by 5% would result in this change:

Volume	R15 750	
Direct cost	R10 500	(67%)
Gross profit	R5 250	

You will have increased your margin by 3% and by so doing lowered the total volume you need to reach break-even.

4.9.2   The goal is profit

You are in business to make a profit, not just to break even. However, by knowing your break-even point, you can manage your business more effectively.

- You can allocate the sales and marketing effort to get you to the point you need to be. For example, you know that you want to sell five extra cars at the end of this month, so you will advertise more than usual.
- You can control costs if you predict a 'slow' month. This happens in most companies, for example the retail industry straight after Christmas. However, losses can be minimised if you plan accordingly. Remember that a few bad months can quickly wipe out accumulated profits.
- You can maximise profits by knowing and understanding the elements of your break-even figure.

4.10   Cash planning: The cash budget (cash forecast)

Up to this point, we have stressed the importance of being able to sustain profits over time.

Important information

Do not attempt any business venture if you cannot sustain profits over time.

Unfortunately, making a profit is not enough. While you must be able to sustain profits over a period of time, it is equally important to have enough cash available to manage the business on a day-to-day basis. You may be making a net profit but lack sufficient ready cash (money) to meet expenses as they occur. If this happens, you cannot continue trading and you will go bankrupt and have to close your business. When you do not have money to meet expenses as they occur, you are in a situation known as technical bankruptcy. So, to continue in business, you must have an adequate cash flow to meet your expenses as they occur.

To overcome this problem, it is extremely important that you pay close attention to the planning of actual money flowing into your business and actual money flowing out. It must be a top priority to know how much actual money you are going to receive and on what dates. You must also know when you have to pay expenses and what amounts are involved. A tool you can use to help with this cash planning is the cash budget.

Definition

The cash budget is a formal plan for forecasting future receipts and payments of cash.

Example

Just as you would not purchase new furniture for your home without enough cash or at least a solid plan to cover a personal loan from your bank, your business needs the same careful handling of its expenditures. All businesses, no matter what type or size, need to develop a plan for their expected cash intake and spending. This is the cash budget.

4.10.1   The purpose of cash budgeting

The cash budget allows you to establish exactly how much cash is flowing into and out of your business. The budget can:

- be used to plan your short-term credit needs
- be presented to your bank or other financial institution to show proper financial planning
- help you predict months when there may be a cash shortfall
- highlight problem areas in your payment schedule—for example, payments to creditors may be lumped together on one date—more careful planning could spread this evenly throughout the entire year.

4.10.2   Consistent budgets

Cash budgeting is a continuous process that can be checked for consistency and accuracy by comparing budgeted amounts with amounts that can be expected from using typical ratios or financial statement relationships. For example, your assessment will estimate the payments made to your suppliers of merchandise or materials, the payments to employees for wages and salaries, and the other payments that you are obligated to make. These payments can be scheduled by date so that you can take advantage of any discounts offered, and so that you will not overlook any of your payments when they become due. Cash collections from customers can also be estimated and scheduled by date along with other expected cash receipts. With careful cash planning, you should be able to maintain an adequate cash balance without holding excessive balances of non-productive cash.

Example

Example of a cash budget
The following is an example of a cash budget for the ABC Company.

Cash budget for 90 days
Beginning cash balance	**R320 000**

Add:
Estimated collections on accounts receivable	R750 000
Estimated cash balances	R250 000
	R 1 320 000

Deduct:
Estimated payments on accounts payable	R800 000
Estimated cash expenses	R150 000
Contractual payments on long-term debt	R150 000
Quarterly dividend	R50 000
	R 1 150 000

Estimated ending cash balance	**R170 000**

4.10.3 Analysis of the example cash budget

Analysis of the financial statements of the ABC Company shows the following.

- The accounts receivable remain at about R500 000 throughout the year. This means there is no seasonal fluctuation in sales.
- The accounts receivable turns over six times a year, or once every 60 days.
- The inventory throughout the year remains at about R800 000 and turns over every 90 days.
- The accounts payable remains at about R400 000 and turns over eight times a year; about once every 45 days.
- There is an accounts receivable collection period of 60 days and an average balance outstanding of R500 000. It appears that R750 000 is the amount that should be collected on the receivables in 90 days.
- Cash sales should amount to about R250 000 if the inventory of R800 000 valued at cost turns over once in 90 days and if the average mark-up is about R200 000. Therefore, if an inventory of R1 000 000 at retail turns over once every 90 days and R750 000 flows through accounts receivable, then approximately R250 000 must be sold on a cash basis.
- Cash payments for expenses are estimated to be R150 000 in the next 90 days. This figure can be roughly checked by referring to the expenses of the income statement. A rough measure of the cash expenses can usually be obtained by using the operating expenses less any non-cash expenses such as depreciation. For example, if there is no seasonal factor, the total amount divided by four should be an approximate check on the amount budgeted for the next 90 days.

4.11 Summary

It should be clear from the discussion that performing a viability study is an integral part of the planning process for any business. We discussed the reason for carrying out such a study and explained the various steps in the process.

When conducting the viability study, it is important to conduct market research to establish exactly who your customers will be, whether there is a real need for the product or service behind your idea, and who your competitors will be. It is also necessary to calculate what your income will be; to do this you need to be able to calculate the cost price of your product or service, calculate the selling price and from those figures establish what your profit will be. You must be able to draw up a cash budget and calculate the break-even point of the business.

The reason behind the viability study has been stressed. Remember, to be viable, your business idea must be profitable and sustainable over a period of time.

Self-evaluation questions

1. Discuss what a viability study is and why it is important.
2. How will you establish whether you have the product or service the customer wants?
3. What kind of information forms part of a customer profile?
4. Define a market for a product of your choice.
5. Name and discuss the questions that need to be asked in order to see whether there is a need for a particular product or service.
6. What is the purpose of a mission statement?
7. What are the questions that need to be answered when formulating the mission statement?
8. Name the characteristics of objectives.
9. Why is it important to calculate the expected market share?
10. What do you need to calculate the expected market share?
11. How can one establish a target market?
12. Define indirect costs.
13. Describe what constitutes manufacturing costs.
14. What is the formula to determine cost per unit for a manufacturing enterprise?
15. What is the formula to determine the total costs of a product for a service enterprise?
16. What is the formula to determine the total costs of a product for a commercial enterprise?
17. Define the break-even point for a business.
18. What is a cash budget?
19. What is the purpose of a cash budget?

References and further reading

'Body to replace Cipro launched'. 2011. http://www.fin24.com/Economy/Body-to-replace-Cipro-launched-20110418 (accessed 7 July 2011).

Cant, M C, Brink, A & Machado, R. 2005. *Pricing Management*, 2nd ed. Claremont: New Africa Books.

Cant, M C (ed). 2010. *Marketing: An Introduction*. Cape Town: Juta.

Cant, M C, van Heerden, C H & Ngambi, H C. 2010. *Marketing Management: A South African Perspective*. Cape Town: Juta.

'Cipro's beginner's guide to our services'. 2011. http://www.cipro.gov.za/products_services/beginners_guide.asp (accessed 28 March 2011).

'New companies act summary'. http://www.adamsadams.com/articles/attorney-law/new-companies-act-summary.html (accessed 28 March 2011).

Nieuwenhuizen, C. 2011. Basics of Entrepreneurship. 2nd ed. Cape Town: Juta.

Strydom, J W (ed). 2004. *Introduction to Marketing*, 3rd ed. Cape Town: Juta.

'The dTi prepares the public for the new consumer protection act'. 2011. http://www.dti.gov.za/mediareleases/consumer_rights.pdf (accessed 28 March 2011).

CHAPTER FIVE

The business plan

Alex Antonites

Learning outcomes

After studying this chapter, you should be able to:

- understand the purpose of a business plan
- identify and describe the potential users of a business plan
- explain the character of a business plan
- understand the preparation phase in writing a business plan
- comprehend the different structures of a business plan
- draft a basic business plan.

5.1 Introduction

In Chapter 4 we discussed the first half of our business planning, namely how to do the viability study. If you have decided that your business idea is indeed viable, then you can move on to the next step: the business plan.

The business plan plays a pivotal role in the entrepreneurial process. If you, as an entrepreneur, apply for start-up capital, a government grant or if you tender for a government contract, one of the first questions you will be asked is if you have a business plan. Your business plan is the platform on which your business will be judged. Remember that the business opportunity is the core focus of entrepreneurial venturing. A business plan is a picture of how the entrepreneur will participate in the entrepreneurial process.

Let us assess two entrepreneurial cases:

Case study

Refilwe Shabang, a first-year informatics student at a local university, developed a web portal where students could buy second-hand academics books. This site is web and mobile enabled. Her thinking behind the business model was that many students want to sell their second-hand textbooks, but do not know how to go about this. At the time, the concept was unique and promised high-income potential for the entrepreneur. Refilwe quit her studies and started the business formally. She spent hours refining the web-based business and spend a lot of money on development and applications to link the seller with the buyer. It was user friendly and became a very popular platform at three leading universities. Students posted their book adverts and also a suggested price. The physical purchasing was the responsibility and arrangement of the buyer and seller, and not that of Refilwe. More than 2000 second-hand books were sold via the site.

Success? No, not at all. This business took long hours to manage and in the end she did not make a single cent! Refilwe did not have a proper income model and in the end offered a free service.

Ntombi opened a small outlet near her home to sell milk. As the sales increased, she realised that an opportunity existed for making yoghurt out of the milk that had not been sold and had date-expired. She decided to expand, and opened a small yogurt factory. Ntombi was then also able to expand her sales area with her new product. Because the business did well, Ntombi could again expand and build a cheese-making unit.

All these decisions were based on well-researched opportunities in the marketplace and on sound financial planning. Because of this planning, and given the vigorous growth of the business, Ntombi is now investigating the possibility of buying a dairy farm.

These are typical scenarios drawn from the lives of emerging modern entrepreneurs. Because of a lack of planning, the first case ends in failure (no income model) whereas the second shows entrepreneurial performance and success. One of the cornerstones of success is in-depth planning; the business plan is an integral part of this planning process. An entrepreneur without a plan is like Facebook without people!

5.2   The purpose and principles of the business plan

The primary objective of the business plan is to develop a blueprint to define your business.

The plan is:

- a detailed written document stipulating how you will address all the business activities to exploit the identified business opportunity
- a planning document that explores and indicates the route to follow into the future
- a document that you, the entrepreneur, should formulate by yourself.

Consider the points discussed below before compiling your plan.

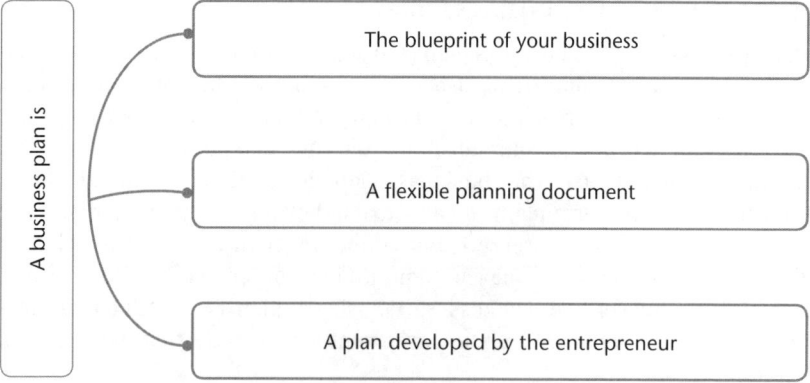

Figure 5.1: The business plan

5.2.1 A blueprint for the business

The business plan serves exactly the same purpose as an architect's plan, which includes a detailed building schedule with quantities and costs of all the items necessary to complete the work, such as bricks, mortar, wood, steel and labour. In the same way, the business plan lists all the facets of the proposed business. A business plan explains exactly what the opportunity is to be pursued and, coupled with that, how the entrepreneur will exploit the opportunity. The roadmap from pre-start to start-up to eventual growth is displayed in a business plan.

5.2.2 A flexible planning document

The business plan is not a static or fixed document; it is a dynamic planning instrument that should be updated regularly to take account of changes in the business environment. For instance, customer buying patterns may shift towards healthier eating (for example, a trend towards low-fat yogurt); new competitors may enter the market with new, comparable products (for example, soya milk yogurt). Your suppliers may also change their approach (for example, no more credit offerings, which could have a negative impact on cash flow). Timely adaptation to these changes is the only way for your business to survive. The digital world has changed the way we conduct business dramatically. Continuous research on the Internet should be part of the process of adaptation and flexible changes.

5.2.3 A plan developed by the entrepreneur

The only way to understand your business properly is to develop your own business plan. This is the best way to end up with a unique plan that suits you and your business. Whilst it is possible to use the services of an external consultant, this may not be as effective and you may end up with an 'off-the-shelf', generic product. A business plan also serves as a management instrument and guideline; the entrepreneur is initially also the manager and requires an operational framework in this regard.

5.3 Other users of the business plan

A secondary objective of the business plan is to acquire finance from a commercial bank or other financial institution. It can also serve as a marketing document to present to potential investors or venture capitalists. The larger suppliers of raw material may also ask to see the plan to evaluate your substance and financial position.

Some entrepreneurs use the business plan to motivate their employees; by communicating the long-term planning and goals, they hope to give their staff a greater sense of 'ownership'. However, there is a certain danger in making your plans known because the core competencies may become known to your competitors if and when employees leave your service businesses. A business plan is a confidential document and anyone who reads it should sign an agreement which states that they will maintain confidentiality.

The following chart summarises the other users of a business plan.

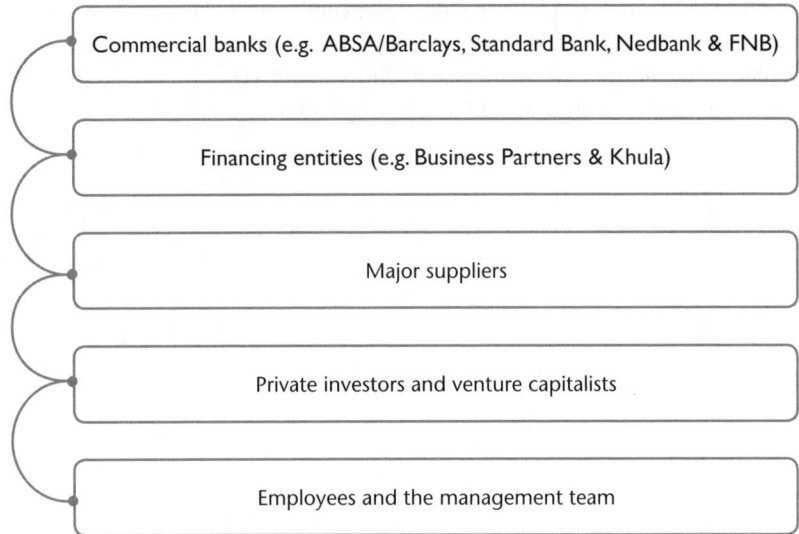

- Commercial banks (e.g. ABSA/Barclays, Standard Bank, Nedbank & FNB)
- Financing entities (e.g. Business Partners & Khula)
- Major suppliers
- Private investors and venture capitalists
- Employees and the management team

Figure 5.2: Potential users of the business plan

5.4 The character of the business plan

What role does the business plan play in starting or growing a business? Wickham (2004) formulated four useful mechanisms in supporting business success. A business plan is a working tool for:

- **Analysis:** A business plan is a document that contains information on each and every variable in the business. The structure, which is the first step in writing the plan, serves as an effective 'checklist' of all the sets of information needed.
- **Synthesis (integration):** The information gathered through using the structure as a guiding principle must now be integrated to make business sense. For example, if you want to advertise in a magazine that reaches your target market, the cost of this should be reflected in the financial plan.
- **Communication:** The plan serves as a communication tool for all the users. It contains valuable information on the nature of the opportunity and also explains how it will be exploited. The bank, for instance, can now see how you will pay back your loan (cash-flow projections).
- **Action:** A business plan without action is like a motorcar without an engine; it has no use. The most difficult task for you, as the entrepreneur, will be to implement your plan. Remember that the plan is a flexible document that should take into account unforeseen conditions and changes in the market and macro environments. It must therefore contain information on methods to implement the planned activities.

Figure 5.3 shows the interaction amongst these characteristics in the context of business success.

The business plan is a planning instrument that shows the entrepreneurial process and describes how the entrepreneur will implement the process. However, it is not the nucleus of success. Many potential entrepreneurs may think that if a business plan is on paper, success will follow. Business success and entrepreneurial performance are dependent on much more. Initially, you would have identified a feasible opportunity in the market environment. As discussed and explained in Chapter 4, you would then have undertaken a viability study. A viable opportunity therefore pre-empts the written business plan. The viability study creates a platform for writing the business plan.

Table 5.1 distinguishes between the opportunity and the business plan.

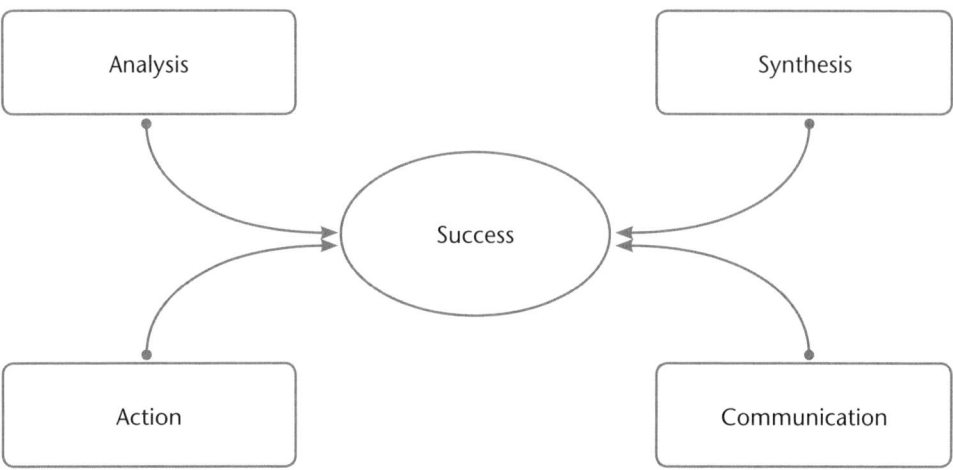

Figure 5.3: The mechanisms of a business plan in supporting business success
Adapted from Wickham (2004)

Table 5.1: From the opportunity to the business plan

Identify and evaluate the opportunity	• Creation and length of opportunity • Real and perceived value of opportunity • Risk and returns of opportunity • Opportunity versus personal skills and goals • Competitive situation
Develop the business plan	• Title page • Table of contents • Executive summary • Description of business • Description of industry • Marketing plan • Financial plan • Production/Operations plan • Organisation plan • Summary
Determine the resources required	• Existing resources available • Resource gaps and available supplies • Access to needed resources
Manage the enterprise	• Management style • Key variables for success • Identification of problems and potential problems • Implementation of control systems

Adapted from Hisrich & Peters (2005)

Important information

Remember that the viability study pre-empts the business plan and contains valuable information to assist with drafting the plan.

Hisrich and Peters (2005) suggest that the following information should be included in your viability study:

- **The proposed location for the business:** Include an assessment on the accessibility of the business for customers, suppliers and distributors.
- **Manufacturing operations:** Decide whether the product/s should be manufactured by yourself or outsourced. If you are going to manufacture the product/s yourself, consider the skills necessary to do so.
- **Raw materials:** Assess the availability, quantity, quality and cost of raw materials.
- **Equipment:** Consider the equipment that is required to manufacture the product effectively and efficiently and also the most suitable way of acquiring this equipment (purchase or lease).
- **Human resource skills:** Detail all the aspects surrounding the human resources requirements (quantity, skills levels, remuneration/cost and the sources of employment).
- **Space:** The optimal size of the factory should be determined and then combined with the cost and availability of manufacturing space (linked to the location decision).
- **Fixed and variable costs:** Analyse all the cost variables surrounding the pre-establishment, start-up and establishment phases of the business (for instance, marketing research, rent, salaries/wages, equipment, lease amounts, insurance, professional fees and advertising).
- **Viability:** The viability study is a decision-making platform for the entrepreneur and serves as a fundamental source of information in drafting an effective business plan. (Refer to Chapter 4 for more on this subject.)

5.5 Pitfalls in writing a business plan

A clear understanding of the audience that will eventually read the business plan is of the utmost importance, as one needs to align the content and core purpose accordingly (eg a venture capitalist will have a different approach to that of a commercial bank in the evaluation process). The first and most important 'audience' is you, the entrepreneur. The first plan should be drafted to serve your specific needs, and thus a roadmap for success. In the process of compiling an appropriate plan for the suitable reader the entrepreneur should address the following pitfalls (dos and don'ts) as conveyed by Timmons and Spinneli (2007: 225):

Table 5.2 The pitfalls to be addressed when compiling your first business plan

Do
1. Involve the entire management team in preparing the plan (if applicable).
2. Make the plan logical, comprehensive, readable and as short as possible.
3. Demonstrate commitment to the venture by investing time in it.
4. Articulate what the critical risks and assumptions are and how you will react.
5. Disclose and discuss any current or potential problems in the venture.
6. Identify several other sources of financing.

7. Remember that the plan is not a business—a kilogram of can-do implementation requires two kilograms of planning.	
8. Know your targeted investment group and what they want in a plan.	
9. Let the realistic market and sales projections drive the assumptions underlying the financial spreadsheets, rather than the reverse.	
Don't	
1. Have unnamed, mysterious people on the management team.	
2. Make ambiguous, vague or unsubstantiated statements.	
3. Describe technical products or manufacturing processes using jargon that only an expert will understand.	
4. Spend money on developing fancy brochures and other 'sizzle'; rather show the 'steak'.	
5. Waste time writing a plan when you could be closing a sale and collecting cash.	
6. Forget that the deal is only done when the cheque clears!	

Also keep the following in mind:

- A business plan is a formal written document.
- It should have a professional 'look and feel' (do a proper spell check).
- The process is time consuming so allow for adequate planning for it.
- Do not rely on Internet-based software that develops the plan for you (it still requires your strategic thinking and application).
- All the components of a business plan should communicate with each other (eg what is mentioned in the marketing plan should be reflected in the financial plan/ projections).

5.6   The structure of the business plan

The structure of a business plan is extremely important. It is advisable to structure your plan so that it meets the needs of your industry and the needs of the potential reader or user. A service-rendering business, for instance, will simply not have a production plan. Business plan structures should be guided by the following basic requirements (Baron and Shane, 2009):

- What is the core idea and its opportunity?
- Why will someone buy or use the product/service?
- How will the idea be operationalised?
- Who is involved in the venture (entrepreneur or team)?
- What is the structure of the new business (strategically and operationally)?

Adapt the structure and style to the needs of the reader, and remember that you will be the first reader and user. The following four basic structures are widely used.

Table 5.3: Structure 1: The comprehensive structure

1. Cover page	
• Name and address of business	• Name of entrepreneur
• Nature of business	• Statement of finance needed (optional)
• Statement of confidentiality of report	

2. Executive summary	

3. Industry analysis	
• Current and potential trends	• Competitive analysis
• Market segmentation	

4. Business description	
• Background of entrepreneur or team of entrepreneurs	• Core product/service
• Unique selling point/s	

5. Production plan	
• Operational process	• Physical outlay of manufacturing facility
• Machinery and equipment	• List of suppliers and their core competencies

6. Marketing plan	
• Pricing	• Distribution
• Promotion	• Sales forecasts

7. Organisational plan	
• Legal form of ownership	• Description of shareholders or members
• Management structure and role description	• Background of managers or project leaders (if applicable)

8. Assessment of risks	
• Assessment of internal weaknesses	• Market risks
• Business risks	

9. Financial plan	
• Projected income statement	• Projected balance sheet
• Projected cash-flow statements	• Break-even analysis
• Sources of finance and the application thereof	

10. Addendum	
• Marketing research information	• Contracts and patents/copyright (if applicable)
• Letters related to the business	

Table 5.4: Structure 2: The general structure

1. Cover page	

2. Executive summary	

3. Business description	
• General description of business	• Industry background
• Primary goals of the business	• Uniqueness of the product/service
• List of suppliers and their core competencies	

4. Marketing plan	
• Marketing research and analysis	• Target market
• Market size	• Competition

• Potential market share	• Marketing strategy
• Pricing	• Advertising and promotions
5. Location	
• Advantages	• Zoning
• Taxes	• Closeness to suppliers
• Transportation issues	
6. Management	
• Management team—key personnel	• Legal structure—shareholding/ membership agreements; employment agreements; ownership
• Board of directors, advisors, consultants	
7. Financial plan	
• Financial forecasting	• Profit and loss
• Cash flow	• Break-even analysis
• Cost controls	• Budgets
8. Critical risks	
• Potential problems	• Obstacles and risks
• Alternative courses of action	
9. Milestone schedule	
• Timing and objectives	• Deadlines
• Relationship of events	
10. Appendices	

Table 5.5: Structure 3: An alternative structure

1. Cover page
2. Executive summary
3. Background and purpose of business
4. Marketing
5. Competition
6. Development, production and location
7. Management
8. Financials
9. Risk factors
10. Harvest or exit

11. Scheduling and milestones
12. Appendices

Table 5.6 Structure 4: Venture capital structure

1. Cover page
2. Company purpose
• Define the company/business in a single declarative sentence
3. The problem
• Describe the exact problem of the customer (or that of the customer's customer)
• Discuss how the customer is addressing the problem currently
4. Solution
• Demonstrate your company's value proposition to make the customer's life better
• Show where your product physically sits
5. Why now?
• Set-up the historical evolution of your solution
• Define recent trends that make your solution possible
6. Market size
• Identify/profile the customer you cater to
• Calculate the size of the market
• Calculate the profitability of the market
7. Competition
• List competitors
• List competitive advantages
8. Product
• Product line-up (form factor, functionality, features, architecture, intellectual property)
• Development roadmap
9. Business model
• Revenue model
• Pricing
• Average account size and/or lifetime value
• Sales and distribution model
• Customer/pipeline list
10. Team
• Founders and management
• Board of directors/Board of advisors
11. Financials
• Income projections
• Balance sheet
• Cash-flow statements
• Capital table
12. The deal

Adapted from http://www.sequoiacap.com/ideas

It must be re-emphasised that the structure of your business plan should be adjusted to the reader. Structure 1 is an all-inclusive plan and suitable to be used as the blueprint of the business; the second and third structures are more general approaches (eg for customers or suppliers) and the last structure is a modern approach that venture capitalists use as a basic framework.

In the case of traditional financing institutions, you will have to adapt to their requirements and proposed structure.

5.7   Guidelines for writing the business plan

The structure and the content of your business plan will be unique to your business. Here are some guidelines to help with writing the actual plan (again link these guidelines to the structure and purpose of the plan).

- **Keep the plan respectably short:** Stick to a concise but clear plan (do not exceed 50 pages).
- **Organise and package the plan appropriately:** Follow a logical structure with a professional presentation (for instance, a cover page with the company name, logo and contact details, presented in such a way that the reader is interested in what is to follow).
- **Orient the plan towards the future:** You should clearly indicate what you intend to do in the future and also include a trend analysis and forecast.
- **Avoid exaggeration:** Do not inflate the potential of the business (for example, be realistic about sales and revenue estimates).
- **Highlight critical risks:** This part shows the reader that you are aware of potential problems and gives you the opportunity to explain ways to manage them.
- **Give evidence of an effective entrepreneurial team:** The management part of the plan is of critical importance as it should convey the skills and contribution of each member of your team to the overall objectives of the business.
- **Do not overdiversify:** The plan should focus only on that segment of the market you identified during your market research (Chapter 4 pages 68–70).
- **Identify the target market:** Give particulars of your target market and explain how you carried out your market research.
- **Keep the plan written in the third person:** Rather use 'he', 'they' or 'them' than 'I', 'we' or 'us'.
- **Capture the reader's interest:** Financial institutions receive many requests for funds. Concentrate on clearly defining the uniqueness of your proposed business.

5.8   Writing the business plan

You are now ready to start writing your plan. As an example, we are going to use Ntombi's Milk Market referred to earlier in this chapter. The full plan forms Appendix A at the back of this book, but a summary of the information that should appear in your plan is covered on the following pages.

5.8.1   Cover page

The cover page should contain the proposed name of the business, its address and relevant contact details. It should also be dated with a date relevant to the content and existence of the plan.

5.8.2 Confidentiality agreement

A business plan contains confidential information on the business make-up, core competencies, competitive advantages and financial condition of the business venture and the entrepreneur. It is therefore critical to safeguard the content by asking the reader/s to sign a confidentiality agreement.

5.8.3 Table of contents

The table of contents guides the reader to the information and should be accurately linked to the content of the plan (insert all the main and sub-headings accompanied by the relevant page number/s).

5.8.4 Executive summary

This summarises the entire plan in two to three pages. It provides the reader with an overview of the status of the business, the basic description of the business and owner/s, potential and current (if relevant) customers, and a brief summary of the financials. It also indicates the purpose of the business plan (for example, financial requirements or investment potential in terms of shareholding). It is advisable to complete the executive summary after the entire business plan has been finalised.

5.8.5 Business description

This section explains in detail exactly what the business intends to do in the market place, in what industry it will operate, the trends and characteristics of the industry and what the business sells or intends to sell to its customers (the unique characteristics of the product/s). Furthermore, it points out the objectives to be achieved in the short, medium and long term.

5.8.6 Marketing plan

The marketing plan illustrates exactly how the product/s will reach the customer. This section highlights the intended target market, what type of media will be used to attract these customers and what pricing strategy will be applied. It also explains the proposed distribution strategy as well as the competition in the selected market. The best way to compile a marketing plan is to base it on proper marketing research findings.

5.8.7 Location

This section of the plan explains why specific decisions were made with regard to the establishment of the business. Such things as the proximity to suppliers and customers, the zoning of the property, as well as transport factors, should form part of this section. Another relevant aspect is the availability of skilled labour as a source for the business. The information contained in this section should be based on the findings of the feasibility study.

5.8.8   Management

This section must show how management will achieve the objectives that have been set for the business. It should illustrate the human competence of the business and include details of the management team and organisational structure (if applicable), the legal structure and available professional support.

5.8.9   Financial plan

The financial plan is to a certain extent the most critical component of the business plan. This section directly specifies what resources are required and how these will be financed and managed. The historical financial performance of the business should be included (in the case of an established entity), or the pro forma or projected financial forecasting in terms of the future expectations. The nature and purpose of the business plan will depict the timeframe of forecasting (for instance, three years or five years ahead). The main body of the financial plan should contain the projected cash flow and income statements as well as balance sheets. A break-even analysis must also support the plan. The example in Appendix A (Ntombi's Milk Market) has a projection of one year only for the cash-flow statements because of limited space. However, it is advisable to do realistic projections over a much longer timeframe (for example, three years).

5.8.10   Critical risks

The risk assessment section must explain all the potential risks that could influence the normal and future operations of the business. These risk factors may be incurred by variables in the macro environment (such as legislation), market environment (such as competition) and micro environment (such as managerial issues). The reader has to understand how the management team will react and manage all the potential threats or risks upon its occurrence. It therefore explores all the 'what if' issues.

5.8.11   Appendices

These should include all the additional detailed documentation as mentioned in the body of the plan, such as:

*   market research
*   curriculum vitae
*   product specifications and photos.

5.9   Summary

Every entrepreneur should remember the saying that 'if one fails to plan, one plans to fail'. A business plan is primarily a planning instrument and blueprint of the business venture, whether new or old. The structure of the plan should be adjusted to the nature of the business and its purpose (for instance, attracting finance). Always keep the reader in mind with specific reference to his or her level of knowledge. The length of the plan is less important than the quality of the content. All the components of the plan should communicate with each other and be strengthened by a well-structured executive summary. Remember, this business tool is flexible and needs continuous adaptation and improvement!

Self-evaluation questions

1. Explain the reason/s for drawing-up a business plan.
2. List three users of the business plan.
3. What is the executive summary?
4. List the critical risks associated with your own business idea.
5. Draft a business plan for your own business idea.

References and further reading

Baron, R A & Shane S A. 2009. *Entrepreneurship: A Process Perspective*, 2nd ed. Mason, OH: Thomson South-Western.

Hisrich, R D, Peters, M P & Shepherd D A. 2005. *Entrepreneurship*, 6th ed. Boston: McGraw-Hill Irwin.

Kuratko, D F & Hodgetts, R M. 2001. *Entrepreneurship: A Contemporary Approach*. Fort Worth: Harcourt College Publishers.

Longenecker, J G, Moore, C W & Petty J W. 2003. *Small Business Management: An Entrerpreneurial Emphasis*. USA: Thomson South-Western.

Nieman, G, Hough J & Nieuwenhuizen, C. 2003. *Entrepreneurship: A South African Perspective*. Pretoria: Van Schaik Publishers.

Timmons, J A & Spinelli, S. 2007. *New Venture Creation: Entrepreneurship for the 21st Century*, 7th ed. Boston: McGraw-Hill.

Wickham, P A. 2004. *Strategic Entrepreneurship: A Decision Making Approach to New Venture Creation and Management*, 3rd ed. Harlow, UK: Financial Times–Prentice Hall.

CHAPTER SIX

Setting up a business

Cecile Nieuwenhuizen

Learning outcomes

After you have studied this chapter, you should be able to:

- identify the legal requirements for establishing a business
- identify the labour legislation that should be considered when establishing a business
- define the factors to be considered when choosing the form of business
- determine the procedures that must be followed to set up a specific form of business
- understand the factors to be considered when choosing the location of a business
- define the essential operating elements of the business functions in the setting-up phase.

6.1   Introduction

You have so far learned:

- how to analyse yourself critically (that is, you have determined your strengths and weaknesses)
- how to turn a business idea into an opportunity for a new business
- how to do a viability study for the proposed business
- how to draw up a business plan.

These were covered in the evaluation and planning phases.

In this final phase, we examine the practical elements of setting up a business.

6.2   The factors that influence the choice of a business form

There are many important factors to consider when choosing the correct business form. The procedure when setting up each form of business is discussed later in this chapter. Many of these are quite complicated and involve particular legal requirements and procedures. It is best to approach an accountant, auditor or attorney before you decide what form your business will take.

A summary of the different forms of business

The sole proprietorship: This is usually a small business owned entirely by one person, who is responsible for supplying the capital and running the business. All the profit belongs to that person but he or she is also responsible for all the losses.

⮑

Partnership: This is where two or more but not more than 20 owners combine their capital and abilities to form a business. The profits and losses are shared among the partners in an agreed ratio. The partners are liable jointly and severally for the debts of the partnership.

Private company: A private company is formed where there is at least one but not more than fifty shareholders. The name of the company must end with the words (Proprietary) Limited or (Pty) Ltd. The business is run by a board of directors, which is elected by the shareholders. Profits are distributed among the shareholders. The liability of each shareholder is limited.

Public company: A public company must have at least seven shareholders. There is no limit on the number of shares issued by the company. Profits are distributed among the shareholders in the form of dividends and the liability of each shareholder is limited to the value of his shares. The name of this business must end with the word Limited. Another difference between a public company and a private company is that the general public can invest in a public company and the number of shares are unlimited. For purposes of this book the public company will not be included as new businesses and small businesses do not make use of the public company as a business form.

Close Corporation (CC): As from 1 May 2011 the Companies Amendment Act of 2008 has been implemented. From this date no new CCs can be registered. However, existing CCs can continue to operate or be sold as CCs until they are changed to private companies. The CC must have at least one owner but not more than ten. No shares are issued and each member's liability is limited unless he is guilty of negligence. The interest of each member is expressed as a percentage. (Table 6.1 contains further information on this topic.)

The new Companies Act will impact on decisions regarding the specific business form that an entrepreneur decides upon. One of the primary implications of the new Companies Act is that specific attention has been paid to the provisions made to small private companies. These provisions are beneficial to the directors of a small business and replace the benefits of a CC. For example, one of the provisions exempts a company from having its annual financial statements audited. In such instances the financial statements of a private company have to be professionally reviewed. This means only companies exceeding a determined size with regard to employees, turnover, debt and shareholding have to be audited. If the aggregate value of the assets of a company are less than R5 million this provision applies (Companies regulations 28(2a), 2011: 34). These provisions are made to limit the cost and time constraints on smaller companies. However, due to demands from shareholders, financiers and boards of directors many smaller companies will audit their statements even though they are exempted.

Table 6.1: The different forms of a business

	Sole proprietorship	Partnership	Private Company	Implications of Companies Act of 2008 on SMMEs	Close Corporation
Number of members	Single individual owner.	Two to twenty people.	One to fifty people.	One to fifty people.	One to ten people.
Establishment procedures	Must be given a trade name. Obtain a trade license.	Relatively simple and can be verbal or in writing.	The incorporation of a company requires certain prescribed documents to be submitted to the Registrar of Companies. The Registrar then issues a Certificate of Incorporation from which moment the company becomes a legal person.	The Act makes provision for new categories of companies, new provisions for minority shareholders and new guidelines for financial statements.	Must be registered by the Registrar of Close Corporations with a written document giving an accounting officer permission to act in this capacity. This is relevant only for existing CCs as no new CCs can be registered.
Liability of members	The owner is personally liable for losses.	The partners are liable jointly and severally for the debts of the partnership.	Limited to paying up their share capital in the company in full.	Provision are made for companies of limited liability where owners of such companies will be protected from personal liability for business debts.	Limited liability for members. However, sometimes members can be personally liable to the corporation for their conduct.
Name of business	No restrictions as long as it is legal.	No restrictions as long as it is legal.	The name must end with the words (Proprietary) Limited/(Pty) Ltd.	The name must end with the words (Proprietary) Limited/ (Pty) Ltd.	The name must end with the letters CC.
Legal entity	This business is not a legal entity. The owner is the legal person.	Not a legal entity.	Has a legal personality and the assets and liabilities of the company are therefore completely separate from those of the shareholders.	Has a legal personality and the assets and liabilities of the company are therefore completely separate from those of the shareholders.	Has a legal personality and its assets and liabilities are its own.

Provision of capital	The owner is responsible for supplying all the capital.	The partners are responsible for supplying all the capital. Their creditworthiness makes it easier to obtain capital.	By making shares available to the shareholders. The general public cannot subscribe to the shares.	By making shares available to the shareholders. The general public cannot subscribe to the shares.	No shareholders; only members who are responsible for supplying the capital.
Distribution of profits	The owner is entitled to all profits.	The profits are shared among the partners in an agreed ratio.	Profits are distributed among shareholders in the form of dividends declared on the number or value of shares held by each shareholder.	Profits are distributed among shareholders in the form of dividends declared on the number or value of shares held by each shareholder.	The members each have an interest in the business expressed as a percentage. Profits are divided according to this percentage.
Continuity	Depends on the owner.	Partnership is dissolved on the death, resignation or insolvency of a partner.	The life is indefinite except when it is liquidated.	The life is indefinite except when it is liquidated.	It exists independently of its members.
Tax	The owner must be registered for tax purposes.	The partnership submits a joint return for the enterprise, but each partner is taxed individually in proportion to what he or she received as profit.	Financial statements must be completed and submitted to the Registrar of Companies. A company is taxed at a fixed rate, which is calculated in accordance with its taxable income.	Low turnover SMMEs can be exempted from complying with the audit requirements.	A close corporation pays its members' salaries. The net income of the close corporation after tax can be distributed to members as dividends. These dividends paid are tax free.
Advantages	Simple to establish. The owner is manager and makes all decisions. All the income belongs to the owner. The owner has a personal interest in the business. It is easy to close down the enterprise.	Easy and inexpensive to establish. Tax is paid separately. Management is determined by the partners and not legislation. Partners have a personal interest. Partners have different skills. Can be dissolved fairly easily.	Is a legal entity. Members have the advantage of limited liability. Existence is not dependent on its members. Because of the number of members the company has more sources of finance.	The Act consolidates the Close Corporations Act of 1984 and the Companies Act of 1973 to make special provision for low turnover SMMEs. Financial statements and record keeping are mandatory which make it possible for SMMEs to apply for funding.	Simple management and decision-making structure. All members are part of management. It is a legal entity. Few legal provisions regulating the establishment and management of the close corporation. Dividends that members receive are not taxable.

	Sole proprietorship	Partnership	Private Company	Implications of Companies Act of 2008 on SMMEs	Close Corporation
Disadvantages	Personally responsible for all debts and liability is unlimited. The owner must supply all the capital. No continuity. Limited knowledge of owner.	Partners have a personal and unlimited liability for the debts of the partnership. Lack of continuity. Problems can arise if partners disagree on the management of the business. Irregularities can occur because it is not necessary to audit the financial statements of the partnership. A partner's conduct can be binding on the partnership even if other partners disagree.	Various additional costs to be paid. Compulsory disclosure of statements and constitution. The company's affairs are known to everyone, including its competitors. Detailed provisions regarding the establishment and management of the company. Employees who do not have shares in the company will not necessarily show the same interest in the company as the owner.	As soon as the company reaches a size as determined by the Companies Act of 2008 the requirements for low turnover SMMEs are the same as for other Private Companies.	Each member can act on its behalf and participate in its management. Selling a member's interest requires approval by all the other members. Limitation to expand due to limitation of ten natural persons. Certain dealings can lead to personal responsibilities. Members limited liability for the debts can make it difficult for the close corporation to obtain credit.

6.2.1   The nature of the product or service

The nature of your product, as well as the complexity of its development, manufacture and marketing, will determine which business form is the most suitable. For example, a business that manufactures security gates requires the involvement of one or two owners, a few employees, possibly a garage to use as a workshop and the minimum of equipment. For this type of business a sole proprietorship or partnership would be sufficient. If, however, you set up a factory to manufacture remote-controlled gates and doors for residential and industrial use, then you should consider a more sophisticated business form, such as a private company because of the larger turnover and sophisticated business setup that is required.

6.2.2   The legal liability of the owners

The close corporation and company possess their own legal personality, while the sole proprietor and the partnership do not. This means that the person in the sole proprietorship and the members of a partnership are usually personally responsible for the tax and debt obligations/commitments of the business. They are therefore personally liable for the commitments of the business.

The shareholders of companies and members of close corporations have limited liability in respect of commitments of the particular business form. The person can therefore be held responsible to a limited extent for the commitments of the company or close corporation.

6.2.3   The business form and the effect of taxation on it

In many cases, the effect of income tax determines the choice of the most suitable business form. The tax policy changes frequently; changes are announced in the annual budget by the Minister of Finance. The current tax rate for companies and close corporations is 28% of profit. The secondary tax on companies (STC) is replaced with a dividends tax at the rate of 10% on dividends paid by companies, with effect from 1 April 2012.

A simplified tax on turnover has been implemented for micro businesses with a turnover of up to R1 million per year as follows:

Taxable turnover	Rate of tax
0–150 000	0%
150 000–300 000	1% of the amount above 150 000
300 001–500 000	1 500 + 3% of the amount above 300 000
500 001–750 000	7 500 + 5% of the amount above 500 000
750 001 and above	20 000 + 7% of the amount above 750 000

These rates are for the year 2011/2012 (ending 29 February 2012) and can change annually or during the course of a year according to the announcement of the Minister of Finance.

6.2.4   Specific legal requirements

You must be aware of the legal requirements for the various business forms. In the case of a company, a Deed of Establishment must be registered with the Registrar of Companies, and financial statements must be drawn up and approved annually by a chartered accountant. According to the Companies Act of 2008 audited statements might not be necessary for low turnover SMMEs.

Certain businesses must renew their licenses annually, for example where health inspectors have to make annual inspections (such as in a restaurant). These are just a few examples of the legal requirements to which you should pay attention.

It is important to collect as much information as possible to determine the most suitable form for your proposed business. You can find information by reading books or making use of experts, such as attorneys, auditors or business consultants. Due to the legal requirements it is recommended that an attorney or auditor is approached for the establishment of a private company. Before a new company can be registered an accounting officer has to be appointed.

6.3   The duties and legal requirements of business forms

The duties and legal requirements that apply to all business forms include the following:

- the person operating the business must have full legal capacity
- the type of economic activity that will be undertaken must be explicitly stated
- the name of the business must be accepted
- the registration of patents, trademarks and designs must be carried out
- testing of products must take place
- licensing must be done
- registration with the Receiver of Revenue must take place
- registration with the Commissioner for Unemployment Insurance must take place
- registration with the Workmen's Compensation Commissioner must take place
- registration with the appropriate local authority must take place
- registration with the Department of Trade and Industry must take place
- the business must comply with general industrial and commercial legislation
- the business must comply with the Act on Occupational Health and Safety.

Each of these requirements is briefly discussed below. The relevant bodies can provide all the information you need; their contact information is included in Appendix B.

6.3.1   *Full legal capacity*

Full legal capacity means that the person who runs the business must be solvent; that is, they must have the capacity to pay their suppliers. An insolvent person or a person under judicial management may not set up a business. The risk involved in entrepreneurship can cause an entrepreneur to lose everything; those who have become insolvent are then prevented by law from establishing a new business while they are insolvent.

6.3.2   *The type of economic activity*

There are different municipal and legal requirements for different types of businesses. For example, a restaurant, bakery or delicatessen has different health requirements to an insurance broker, bottle store or construction company. Find out which legal obligations you have to fulfil from your local municipality or licensing authority.

6.3.3   Naming the business

The law governing business names limits the choice. The trading name of a business must be approved to protect existing businesses and avoid duplication. Company names must be approved by the Registrar of Companies. The choice of a name must comply with the requirements of the Business Names Act (No. 27 of 1960). (Proprietary) Limited/(Eiendoms) Beperk or (Pty) Ltd/(Edms) Bpk must appear at the end of the name of a private company (refer to Table 6.1).

6.3.4   Registration of patents, trade marks and designs

Anyone can patent a unique product, service, trade mark or design. Registration of such a patent is performed by a patents attorney. An annual registration fee is payable after three years so that the registered patent does not expire.

There is a general impression that the cost of registering a patent is restrictive. In South Africa, this cost can be less than R10 000 (this could rise with increasing technical complexity). Foreign patent protection will cost between R20 000 and R30 000.

It may be worthwhile considering patenting a unique product; you would be extremely disappointed if your competitor saw the value in your product and beat you to the patent office.

Trade marks can be registered at the Trade Marks office in Pretoria. A design which gives exclusive rights to form and colour combinations, among other aspects, can be registered with the Designs Office. Registered trade marks are valid for ten years. After this period a Trade Mark can be renewed.

6.3.5   Testing

Products can be tested by the South African Bureau of Standards (SABS). Some companies add a clause to their contracts which specify that products must be manufactured in accordance with the specifications of the SABS.

6.3.6   Licensing

The purpose of the Business Act (No. 71 of 1991) is mainly to ensure deregulation; in other words, to reduce regulations to the minimum. This is to make it easier to establish a business. Approach the local authority to find out the rules and regulations regarding licensing in your area.

6.3.7   Registration with the Receiver of Revenue

You must register your new business with the Receiver of Revenue and you must pay tax as an employer, as a taxpayer and on added value (VAT).

*   **As employer:** The business must collect tax from the employees and pay it to the Receiver, for example SITE (Standard Income Tax on Employees) and PAYE (Pay-As-You-Earn).
*   **As taxpayer:** The business or the owner (depending on the type of business under discussion) must pay tax on net income annually. Businesses make provision for income tax by the payment of provisional tax.

- **Value Added Tax (VAT):** Businesses that have an annual turnover of more than R1 million must register with the Receiver of Revenue for payment of value-added tax (VAT). However, voluntary registration for VAT is possible for businesses making taxable supplies between R50 000 and R1 million. You must obtain information concerning the calculation and payment of VAT before you set up a business. Thorough planning and administration of the business can avoid fines and other problems.

Important information

Value-added tax is based on the following principles:

- VAT must be included in the **selling price** of your product or service and paid by your customers. The business therefore receives VAT on **sales**.
- When a business manufactures products and/or services, the business pays for raw materials, other material, products and services to make the manufacturing and provision possible. The business therefore pays VAT on **purchases**.
- The difference between the **VAT that has been paid** and the **VAT that has been collected** must be paid monthly by the business to the Receiver of Revenue, or claimed back.

Consult an accountant or the local Receiver of Revenue for information on the registration of employees, the provision for the payment of income tax and the payment and claiming of VAT. These consultants can be reached at www. sars.gov.za. You may also want to read the *Tax Guide for Small Businesses* at this website.

6.3.8   *Registration for unemployment insurance*

An employer is obliged by the Unemployment Insurance Act (No. 30 of 1966) to make contributions to the Unemployment Insurance Fund. Employees in the lower income groups qualify in terms of this law for payment of unemployment insurance by the employer. When employees resign, are dismissed or take maternity leave, they are assured of a monthly income for a certain number of months.

6.3.9   *Registration with the Workmen's Compensation Commissioner*

Example

A business must register as an employer with the Workmen's Compensation Commissioner **within 14 days** of commencing business.

Registration is compulsory in terms of the Workmen's Compensation Act (No. 30 of 1941) (as amended). Employees in a particular income group are compensated when, as a result of an accident or injury, they can no longer earn an income. Employers pay the Workmen's Compensation Commissioner an annual amount calculated according to the income of the employees.

6.3.10   Registration with local authorities

Businesses may have to pay service levies and turnover levies to the local authorities. The service levy is a percentage of the amount that is paid in salaries and wages, and the turnover levy is a percentage of the turnover of the business.

6.3.11   Registration with the Department of Trade and Industry

A new manufacturing business must register with the Department of Trade and Industry. Businesses that require import permits are also obliged to register with this Department.

6.3.12   General industrial and commercial legislation

Businesses must comply with the applicable industrial legislation, for example the Occupational Health and Safety Act that provides guidelines on the duties and responsibilities of employers, employees and other persons regarding health and safety compliancy in a business. The Wage Act prescribes minimum wages in cases where industrial agreements do not exist. The Consumer Protection Act (CPA) 68 of 2008 aimed at preventing exploitation of consumers and ensuring fair business. The long list of obligations and legal requirements can be discouraging. However, remember that registrations are mostly done once only and that the contact people at the relevant offices are usually experts and have all the necessary information at their disposal.

6.4   Labour legislation

Most small businesses depend on employees. Therefore knowledge of, and adherence to, labour legislation is important when you start your own business. Labour legislation balances the power between employers and employees and is intended to protect both parties in the employment relationship. The legislation pertaining to this relationship is extensive, and there is unfortunately not enough space here to discuss all of it in detail. However, you can easily obtain the relevant Acts (see Appendix B for telephone numbers and addresses). In this section, we will look at each Act briefly to ensure that you have a basic awareness of relevant legislation.

6.4.1   Employment contracts

In an employment contract the employee makes his or her services available to the employer. The employer describes the duties to be performed by the employee and they agree on a wage or salary. The employer/employee relationship comprises certain rights and obligations that must be mutually agreed. The contract defines whether employment is for a fixed or indefinite period. There are three forms of contract:

- written contracts
- verbal contracts
- tacit contracts.

Written contracts

The duties and obligations of the employer and employee are included in a written contract, for example:

- remuneration
- leave (annual, sick, maternity or other)
- working hours
- protection of the interests of the company (for example, restraint of trade clauses)
- job title and position
- medical aid
- pension fund membership.

The Basic Conditions of Employment Act (No. 75 of 1997) determines specific requirements with regard to employment contracts. The Act requires that at least 20 particulars, as stipulated in Section 29, must be reflected in your contract.

For detailed information, a copy or a summary of the Basic Conditions of Employment Act can be obtained from the address in Appendix B or from www.labour.gov.za.

Verbal contracts

This type of contract is a verbal agreement between the employer and employee. Although verbal contracts are binding, they are not recommended because in a dispute judgement has to be made on the word of one person against another.

Tacit contracts

The terms of the contract and conditions of employment are determined by the past behaviours of the employer and employee respectively. This situation is not advisable because past behaviour might not be interpreted in the same way by the employer and the employee.

Example

Let us look at an example: an employee is employed at a specific salary as a full-time employee, but due to a low workload, eventually works half-days only without a reduction in salary. After a year the situation at the business changes and the employer expects the employee to work a full day at the salary agreed upon when the appointment was made. The tacit agreement of working half-days only can be seen as binding by the employee and he or she can dispute the employer's changed expectations of reverting to full-day work.

6.4.2 Labour Relations Act (No. 66 of 1995)

The Labour Relations Act (LRA) aims to establish co-determination in the workplace. The aim is to transform the relationship between management and labour from being adversarial to being co-operative, from having fragmented dealings with one another to ongoing interaction, and from distributive to a more integrative approach.

The complete Act can be obtained at www.labour.gov.za.

The primary objectives of the Act are to:

- regulate the fundamental rights of all South Africans
- promote collective bargaining and collective agreements
- promote participation of workers in the workplace
- promote the resolutions of disputes.

Regulation of fundamental rights

This section of the Act refers to:

- Freedom of association, which guarantees the rights of employees and employers to form or belong to a trade union or employers' organisation. They may then also participate in the lawful activities of these organisations, participate in elections and be elected as office-bearers or officials.
- Organisational rights, which means the right of the trade union with regard to:
    o access to the workplace
    o deductions of trade union levies from members' wages
    o reasonable leave for trade union activities for office-bearers during working hours
    o disclosure of some information.

The employees are protected against:

- unfair dismissal (Sections 185–197), which determines that an employee can be dismissed for a valid reason only, and a fair procedure has to be followed
- unfair labour practice (Schedule 7, Part B), which includes promotion, demotion, discrimination and disciplining of employees
- strikes and lockouts (Sections 64–77), which refers to the right of employees to strike and of employers to lock employees out.

Promotion of collective bargaining (Sections 23–63)

The Labour Relations Act aims to promote constructive co-operation between management and labour and includes:

- collective agreements
- agency shop agreements
- closed shop agreements
- collective bargaining beyond the workplace
- establishment, powers and functions of bargaining councils
- statutory councils.

Promotion of worker participation (Sections 78–94)

This enables workers to participate in the running of a business through negotiations, institutionalised consultation and joint decision-making.

Workplace forums can be formed only in businesses with more than 100 employees.

Promotion of dispute resolution

The Labour Relations Act (LRA) promotes resolution of disputes at the business level, but provides procedures and support structures for the resolution of labour disputes through conciliation, mediation and arbitration.

The Commission for Conciliation, Mediation and Arbitration (CCMA) was established in terms of Section 112 of the LRA. It is independent of government, political parties, trade unions, employers, employees' organisations, trade union federations or employers' organisations.

The functions of the CCMA are to:

- resolve through conciliation any disputes between an employer and employee referred to it in terms of the LRA

- arbitrate disputes not resolved through conciliation, if determined to do so by the LRA and all parties involved
- assist in the establishment of workplace forums
- compile and publish information and statistics about its activities.

6.4.3 Basic Conditions of Employment Act (No. 75 of 1997)

The purpose of the Act is to give effect to the right to the fair labour practices referred to in section 23(1) of the Constitution. This is done by establishing and making provision for the regulation of basic conditions of employment. The Basic Conditions of Employment Act provides for the right to reasonable and fair minimum conditions of employment.

The most important provisions of the Act are:

- a 45-hour working week (Section 9) and procedures to achieve a 40-hour working week
- maximum over time (Section 10) of three hours a day and ten hours a week
- rate for over time (Section 10 [2]) to be paid at one-and-a-half times the normal wage
- rest period (Section 15) of at least 12 consecutive hours daily
- Sunday work (Section 16) to be paid at double the normal rate
- special provisions and overtime rates for night work (Section 17)
- paid leave (Section 20[1][a]) set at 21 consecutive days after 12 months set at:
  o one day for every 17 days worked
  o one hour for every 17 hours worked
- proof of incapacity with a medical certificate (Section 23)
- maternity leave (Section 25) set at four months, with a possibility of the Unemployment Insurance Fund financing this leave
- family responsibility leave (Section 27) set at three days per year, after being employed for four months
- notice of termination (Section 37)
- written particulars of employment (Section 29). The Act requires that at least 20 particulars, as stipulated in Section 29, must be reflected in your contract.

6.4.4 Employment Equity Act (No. 60 of 1998)

The purpose of the Act is to eliminate unfair discrimination by providing equal opportunities, fair treatment in employment and affirmative action in appointments and promotion.

The Act prohibits discrimination against employees and job applicants on the basis of race, gender, pregnancy, marital responsibility, ethnic or social origin, sexual orientation, age, disability, HIV status, religion, conscious belief, political opinion, culture, language and birth.

Affirmative action determines that suitably qualified applicants/employees from the following designated groups should be employed/promoted:

- Black Africans
- Coloureds
- Asians
- women
- the disabled.

6.4.5   Skills Development Act (No. 97 of 1998)

The aim of the Skills Development Act is to ensure that the education, training and development needs of employees are addressed by employers. Employers have to pay a Skills Development Levy of 1% of their annual wages and salaries to the National Skills Fund. When employees are trained or receive education, according to specifications, a percentage (up to 40% of the 1% paid) of their contribution will be paid back to the business. Only those small businesses with a total salary and wage bills of more than R500 000 per year are required to pay the Skills Development Levy.

6.4.6   Black Economic Empowerment (BEE)

The Broad Based Black Economic Empowerment (BBBEE) Act (No. 53 of 2003) provides a more inclusive definition of BEE. It includes criteria such as ownership, management and control, employment equity, skills development, affirmative procurement, enterprise development and social development. It also provides for transformation charters for the various sectors of the economy. According to the BBBEE Act all businesses, including SMMEs, must plan for and implement through a scorecard the basic framework against which to benchmark the BEE process in the business. Strategic representation of previously disadvantaged groups, employment equity and skills development are important matters and should be taken into consideration to ensure survival in any business.

6.5   The procedure when setting up each form of business

In this section, we will look at the different procedures to follow for setting up the various forms of business.

6.5.1   The sole proprietorship and the partnership

Few legal requirements govern the setting up of a sole proprietorship and a partnership.
   The laws and regulations discussed in Section 6.3 apply to these businesses.
   A partnership is formed by a written or oral agreement between the partners. If the partners sign a written agreement, the Stamp Duties Act (No. 77 of 1968) provides that the contract must be stamped.

6.5.2   The company

The Companies Act of 2008 amended from a combination of the Companies Act (No. 61 of 1973) and the Close Corporations Act (of 1984) prescribes the way to form a company. Note that major changes have been implemented in the Companies Act of 2008, as discussed in this chapter and Chapter 4. The registration and creation of a company is performed by the office of the Registrar of Companies in Pretoria.
   The steps in setting up a company are:

- **Reserve a name for the company:** This is to ensure that the name is not already being used by another company and avoids misrepresentation. The name must also by law be acceptable to the Registrar of Companies. A specific form of the Companies Act is used for this purpose.

- **A Memorandum of Association and Statutes/Articles must be drawn up:** A chartered accountant or attorney can be appointed to do this. Each signatory of the Memorandum of Association receives a certain number of shares and the number of shares is recorded alongside the name of the signatory. There is only one shareholder in a one-person company. The signatories to the Memorandum of Association also sign the statutes.

The following documents and information must be submitted to the Registrar of Companies for the registration of a company:

- Details of the reserved or approved name, the translation of the name or a shortened form, if applicable.
- Two copies of the Memorandum of Association and Statutes that have been signed as prescribed, over and above the original Memorandum of Association and Statutes.
- Information concerning the situation of the registered office and postal address (also a form of the Companies Act).
- Written acceptance by a chartered accountant that he/she is prepared to audit the annual financial statements for companies with higher turnovers.
- Annual duty of a fixed amount must accompany the application at registration.
- Proof that the registration fee has been paid.

The Registrar of Companies endorses a certificate that the company has been incorporated. The Certificate of Incorporation indicates that the company has received a legal personality.

6.5.3 The close corporation

As from 1 May 2011 there is no provision for the registration of new Close Corporations.

6.6 Factors that play a role in the choice of location

There are many factors that play a role in identifying a suitable location for your business. It is a good idea to read widely on the topic, to make enquiries and ask experts for advice. Consider the following when choosing a location.

- **The market:** This is especially important in the case of a trading enterprise where the business must be visible and accessible to the target market.
- **Access to raw materials:** This is particularly important to manufacturing businesses. You should consider whether it is more important to be close to the market or close to raw materials. The type of raw materials and the type of final product will determine this choice (for example, in the case of a roof sheeting manufacturer, the factory should be built near a power station so that the heaps of coal ash do not have to be transported too far).
- **Human resources/labour:** Ensure that you will be able to employ suitable human resources, with the correct skills with people who live in the area.
- **Costs:** Compare the cost of renting/buying premises in different locations and compare these with your competitor's costs. Remember that the cheapest is not always the best.
- **Climate:** As an example, consider that your business produces leather outfits for men and ladies. This type of business would no doubt sell more outfits if it is located in Cape Town (which has cold and wet winters) than in Durban (where temperatures remain moderate even during the winter).

- **Regional incentive programmes:** To encourage development in particular regions or industries, the government offers industrial incentive schemes. These entail, for example, the availability of financing for building factories in certain areas, reduced taxation for a specific period, grants for businesses in the tourism industry, and so on. Contact the Department of Trade and Industry and your local authorities for more information.
- **Services:** Take note of the availability of services such as public transport systems, water supply, parking space, electricity and the support services of other businesses in the area that you are considering.
- **Personal and social considerations:** These are often the most important factors in the choice of a location. Consider whether the premises will be close enough to where you live to make them convenient for you.

Finally, remember that location is a very important consideration when opening a business, as it will have a huge influence on competitiveness. You must conduct thorough market research before signing a rental or purchase agreement and also seriously consider seeking professional advice from an attorney before signing.

Remember that it is possible to negotiate a rental agreement that will be more beneficial for the business; you do not have to accept the first set of terms offered by the estate agent or owner of the premises. Here you should be well informed of your rights according to the Consumer Act 68 of 2008.

6.7 Setting-up factors that are related to the business functions

A large variety of activities occur within a small business in the process of providing goods and/or services. These activities can be systematically divided into smaller groups by placing similar activities together. Each group of activities is called a function. We can identify eight interdependent functions, namely:

- The marketing function is responsible for all activities related to supplying the consumer with the products or services provided by the business.
- The public relations function is the promotion of a positive impression of the business in the external environment.
- The information and record systems function involves the control of information systems in the business to ensure that information is obtained, processed and made available to management.
- The financial function involves budgeting and the effective application of funds and the use of finance.
- The human resource function includes the effective use of employees.
- The purchasing function is responsible for the timely purchasing of goods and services at the right price, of the required quality and quantity from suppliers.
- The operational function is responsible for transforming inputs such as raw materials, labour and finance into outputs—the products or services that the business offers.
- The general management function includes all the activities that lead the business to achieve its objectives and is found in each of the functions of a business. The general management function consists primarily of the activities of planning, organising, leading and control.

Together, the eight functions represent all the activities performed in a business. In the following sections we take a look at what must be done in respect of the business functions when a business is set up. The eight business functions are discussed separately, but there is a degree of overlap.

6.7.1 The marketing function

As you saw in the example of the business plan in Chapter 5, it is important to plan your marketing campaign. Consider the target market, the variety of products and/or services that will be made available, at what price and how and where they will be made available (distribution). This is the core of the marketing plan.

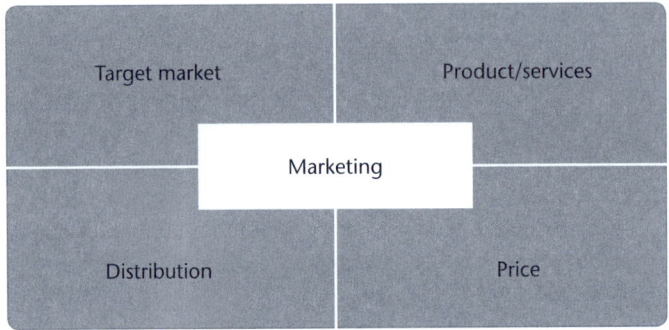

Figure 6.1: The core of the marketing plan

The marketing plan therefore provides answers to the following questions:

- Where are we now?
- Where do we want to be?
- How do we get there?
- How do we exercise control?

Consumer Protection Act of 2008

With regard to the marketing of your business you must also be sure that the business delivers what you promise in the marketing process. Consumers are protected by the Consumer Protection Act by provisions such as:

- the right to fair marketing
- the right to return goods and get refunds
- the right of a six-month warranty on all products bought and
- strict liability, giving the consumer the right to sue if goods cause injury or damage.

Name, logo and motto

By this stage you will have finalised a name for your business and settled on a motto. The motto is a brief description in a few words that encapsulates the ethos or ideals of your business.

Example

Avis (the car rental company) uses the motto 'We try harder'.
Standard Bank's motto is 'Moving forward.'

Once you have decided on the name (and possibly registered it with the Registrar of Companies) you should not change it because as your product or service becomes associated with that name, it becomes a valuable marketing tool.

It is also a good idea to have a logo graphically designed that reflects the name and mission statement of your business. You can use this logo, and possibly the mission statement, on your letterheads, business cards, invoices and any other business stationery.

Example

Example

Remember that the abbreviations CC or (Pty) Ltd and the company registration number must always appear on stationery.

The names of members (for a CC) and directors (for a (Pty) Ltd) must also appear on stationery.

Form of communication

Consider the best form of communication to market your business. Think about where and how your competitors advertise, and in what other ways they market their products. Then consider the same advertising channels, but remember to distinguish your advertisements from those of competitors in a significant way. For the small business, personal sales are an important method of communication. Personal sales are where prospective customers are contacted personally or by word of mouth; also when satisfied customers recommend the business to their network of friends, family and acquaintances.

The Internet is one of the most prominent ways to advertise your business. A web page designed for your business is also a relatively cost effective way of advertising a new business.

The cost of advertising is high. Therefore it is a good idea to develop a method of monitoring the results of each advertisement. In this way you can determine their cost-effectiveness.

Example

An example is a person who gives quotations for garden services by appointment. When prospective customers call to make the appointment, find out how they heard of your business. In this way, the 'hit-rate' on each advert can be established.

You should also take note of the sales each advert generates. Remember that there are certain days of the week when your customers will be able to respond to an advert more easily.

Example

For example, an employment agency will advertise positions in the local or a national newspaper at the beginning of the year rather than before the December holidays, or during the term rather than during holidays or long weekends, as job seekers react better at certain times of the year. Restaurants will focus their advertising on periods when their customers are more likely to dine out, for example over weekends and around the end of the month around pay days, when prospective customers will be more likely to have money available for entertainment.

6.7.2   The public relations function

Try as far as possible to make use of public relations to promote the image of your business. In public relations the image of the business as a whole is important. The goals of public relations include the creation of goodwill, mutual understanding, acceptance and co-operation with interested parties of the business. Do not confuse this with marketing, which is responsible for promoting specific products or services.

Here are some hints on promoting public relations:

- Make use of acquaintances and friends who can make your business known; in other words, make use of your network of people and friends (through the process called 'networking').
- Invite journalists from the local newspaper to the opening of the business.
- Ask for an article to be written about your business when you are placing advertisements in a publication.
- Write an article yourself and send photographs with it for publication if someone from the press cannot be present.

It is important to use creative and even alternative methods of exposure to make your business known and to distinguish it from similar businesses.

Example

The following is a good example of successful public relations.

Mary Jacobs opened an exclusive coffee shop in her home and publicised the opening by sending personal invitations to the press, prospective clients, their friends and colleagues. The opening lasted for three days and guests were entertained free of charge. The launch was personal, the refreshments and the service excellent and gave a foretaste of the quality of the coffee shop. After the introductory period, many people were aware of the coffee shop, with the result that a strongly representative group of the target market now visits the coffee shop regularly and the owner can rely on personal recommendations.

Testimonials from satisfied clients are also excellent forms of external relations. Ensure that clients have the opportunity to give feedback on their experience with your business, for example by filling out a 'customer comments section' on your web page.

Relevant organisations and associations can be beneficial for promoting your business. Local chambers of commerce as well as business and sports clubs are just a few examples of where valuable contacts can be built up.

6.7.3   *The information and record systems function*

From the first day your business starts trading, records of relevant information must be kept. It is important to develop an effective and user-friendly record-keeping system.

Some examples and requirements of record-keeping systems are:

- a system for keeping information on clients (client information) available
- an accounting system that you understand and that is simple and effective
- an effective stock control system
- a system for the control of cash
- a system for keeping records of marketing, enquiries and sales
- a record of turnover and profit for tax purposes and, among others, for levies to local authorities.

The kind of information you must record will determine which filing system is the most effective. Customers for whom specifications and other documentation and information sheets must be kept will warrant a file for each client, stored in a steel cabinet and arranged alphabetically. An example is a town and regional planner who opens a file for each project/client and keeps everything, such as maps and plans relating to that job, in it. On the other hand, a card system will be sufficient for clients if you only need to store client's personal information. A hairdresser or beautician would use such a card system, for example.

Information and filing systems are available for computers in, for instance, Microsoft Office, or specialist programmes such as the VIP payroll programme for businesses which use payrolls. Information of most businesses is computerised although some functions might not be computerised, such as personal files of employees.

6.7.4   *The financial function*

When you conducted your viability study (discussed in Chapter 4), you would have determined:

- what capital is required to set up the business
- how the capital requirement will be financed.

Financing your business

It is important that you use some personal funds for a portion of the initial capital before approaching a bank for financing. Financing institutions generally require a certain amount of own investment to show that you, as the entrepreneur, are committed to the business and motivated to achieve success.

Ensure that you obtain the right finance for your requirements.

Example

For a fixed asset such as a hotel, you would most likely need a large amount of money to add to your own investment. For this, you would need long-term financing.

For smaller and less costly assets such as computer equipment, you would need only short-term financing. It is also desirable to pay off computer equipment quickly, because it becomes technologically outdated very quickly.

Different financial institutions specialise in specific areas. Financial institutions such as Business Partners, the Industrial Development Corporation, the small, medium and micro enterprise (SMME) sections of banks and development corporations (such as Ithala in KwaZulu-Natal), can provide financing to address the needs of SMMEs. Financing ranges from direct loans to incentive schemes, and programmes can be adapted to your specific requirements.

Example

Khula, the wholesale finance division of the Department of Trade and Industry, makes finance available to small, medium and micro enterprises through various retail financial intermediaries, including NGOs and banks. The aim of Khula's credit guarantees is to provide access to finance for SMME owners who might not qualify for finance through normal banking channels. Khula financial schemes require lower collateral and a lower percentage of owner funds. Khula will also be providing finance directly to businesses from 2011.

Example

Funders can also be approached. For example, Acorn Technologies, a government-funded incubator for companies in the life science arena, has developed a website which aims to link suitable investors with entrepreneurs or companies that need financing to start or expand their businesses. See the interactive website www.fundman.co.za for more information and an extensive and searchable database of fund providers in South Africa, including their investment criteria and contact details.

For more information on financing your business and other related matters, such as incentive schemes, tender opportunities and new business opportunities, the website of the Business Referral and Information Network (BRAIN), at www.brain.org.za, covers everything of interest to the small business entrepreneur.

Managing your finances

You should consider the following points.

- **Develop a basic accounting system:** This does not have to be complicated but it must meet the needs of your business and you must be able to understand it.
- **Appoint an external bookkeeper or accountant:** Do this if you do not wish, or are not able, to handle the bookkeeping yourself. The money that you pay for this service will be worth it. For the small business it is sometimes possible to share an

accountant with other businesses. Such a person will need to spend one or two days a week or month to do your business's accounts.

- **Draw up specific cash budgets (as discussed in Chapter 4):** This is part of the planning for the next period. Adjust the budgets if necessary. Budgets are important, because they can give you an indication of when cash will be available and when cash-flow problems may be experienced. They are essential for planning and are also useful for the control of business activities.
- **Maintain a good relationship with your bank:** To obtain additional capital and to ensure a positive attitude on the part of the bank manager, it is important to meet your obligations punctually. If this is not possible for some reason or other, explain the situation to the bank manager so that alternative arrangements can be made. An informed bank manager contributes to a sound relationship.
- **Insurance:** Make provision for the insurance of stock, vehicles, contents of your office, contracts, equipment, buildings, etc.
- **Creditworthiness:** If you sell on credit, make sure you check the creditworthiness of your customers. This can be done by asking customers to supply trade references and banking details. Information can also be obtained at a price from credit bureau. Determine beforehand on what terms credit will be granted (for example 60 days) and stick to them.
- **Keep up to date with economic affairs:** Read financial magazines and the business section of the newspaper for this information. It is particularly important to be aware of economic factors such as interest rates and inflation.

6.7.5   The human resources function

In order to plan your staffing requirements and ensure that you make sound appointments, consider the following points:

- Draw up a list of all the tasks that must be performed in the business.
- Group the tasks so that tasks that can be performed by a specific person can be combined. This combination of tasks is the job description.
- Determine what qualifications and skills the person must have to perform the tasks. These are the job specifications of the appointment.
- Then recruit the right people. This can be done by:
  - placing an advertisement, conducting the interviews and reference checking yourself
  - using a recruitment agency (they charge a fee equal to 7–15% of an appointment's annual salary)
  - approaching training organisations such as schools, technical colleges or tertiary institutions where teachers or lecturers can make recommendations.
- When you are looking for people with specific personal characteristics and attributes for a demanding or specialised position it is also good to do psychometric evaluation through an industrial psychologist to determine whether the candidate possesses the required attributes.

Once you have found the right candidate, draw up an employment contract. (The employment contract is discussed under 6.4.1.) Make sure you give your new employee a clear, written job description when you sign the employment contract together.

Important information

Think carefully before appointing family or friends, as this has many pitfalls. You may be tempted to make such an appointment because it is the quickest or easiest method of appointment, or to help a friend/family member, or because the person has a specific characteristic that is clearly favourable for the business.

However, doing this means that you do not compare the person with other suitable candidates for the post. Examples of complications include:

- he or she does not have the necessary skills or qualifications
- personal and working relationships differ
- friction can arise, with adverse effects for the business
- jealousy of the family member or friend towards you, the employer, due to personal involvement
- family appointments and promotions can make other employees jealous
- friction between other family members and friends.

6.7.6 The purchasing function

Find out about trade and speciality shows. You can make purchases at shows, and obtain information about innovations and product developments in your area of business. You can also market your products at these shows.

Example

Examples are the South African Retailers, Dispensaries and Chemist Association (SARDCA), which is an annual show where wholesalers in gifts, household goods, interior decorations and general retail products display their products to retailers and service providers. Buyers view a large variety of available products under one roof and can place orders with various wholesalers. Similar shows are arranged for the catering, jewellery, construction, beauty, interior decorating, antique collectors and fashion industries.

Consider the following points when setting up your purchasing function:

- Negotiate with suppliers for better prices for cash, to obtain products on consignment or for 30-day accounts. The financial planning of the business will determine what is the most favourable method of payment for purchases.
- Compare suppliers not only in terms of price but also in terms of quality and the services they provide, such as delivery and installation.
- Keep stock to a minimum and control it properly, because carrying stock costs money. The 'Just-in-Time' (JIT) system is an effective stock-control system that was originally developed in Japan. Stock is delivered just-in-time for use to limit the costs of carrying stock. However, it is essential to have sufficient stock on hand for sound customer service.
- Be careful not to become too dependent on one supplier. This can cause problems when this supplier is out of stock, prices become too high or service deteriorates. Find, and also make use of, alternative suppliers to ensure continuous good service. Obtain price lists, information on discounts and catalogues from various suppliers.

- Cultivate good relationships with suppliers. This ensures better service and is especially important when, for instance, raw materials are in short supply, when your supplier may give you preferential treatment.

6.7.7 The operational function

Regarding operations you should consider some or all of the following points:

- Meticulous planning in respect of machinery and other equipment is important so that you do not invest too much capital in it and to ensure optimal use. At the same time, it is essential to make provision for sufficient equipment to ensure timely production or service provision.
- Trained labour to ensure correct use of equipment.
- Expert design/knowledgeable layout of production facilities.
- Cost control to ensure a profitable operation.
- Built-in control measures like inspections and operational procedures.
- Production time. Clients' orders must be executed as agreed and this requires careful planning of equipment and labour.
- 'Bottlenecks' often occur when specialised labour and expensive equipment is involved. Sound planning is essential to avoid bottlenecks so that deliveries can be made on time.
- Outsourcing certain functions in the production process is an option, for example to:
  - Eliminate specific bottlenecks. A building contractor will, for example, make use of subcontractors for carpentry in a certain contract when he/she is already making optimal use of the carpenters in his/her service.
  - Postpone the purchase of expensive equipment. A business that manufactures doors and windows with aluminium frames will initially buy the door handles and window catches from a supplier. When sufficient profit has been made, it can purchase the equipment for making them.
  - Ensure the availability of labour. A nursery will refer clients who are interested in a professionally designed garden to an independent, expert landscape architect. The nursery can offer this service to clients without being responsible for paying the person's salary. It can even make an agreement with the landscape architect that he/she will buy all the plants and supplies from the nursery.

6.7.8 The general management function

As an entrepreneur, you will be the manager of your business during its establishment stage. You will therefore be responsible for:

- formulating goals for the business
- encouraging people to achieve these goals
- performing the management functions of planning, organising, leading and control.

As manager, you will also be responsible for the effective co-ordination of the business functions.

You may appoint an outside person to perform a specific business function, such as a marketing manager who would be responsible for the entire marketing function on a part-time basis. You may also wish to outsource some functions.

> ## Example
>
> Consider the interior decorator who outsources the operations function. He or she does not manufacture the products for the clients, but has it done by different contractors. The overall responsibility for management, however, remains with the decorator, who must ensure that the business functions as a profitable whole.

Outsourcing is a good alternative when you do not have the skills to carry out all the functions. This ensures cost-effectiveness and makes effective management possible.

It is also a management function to determine the optimal operating capacity of the business. A business reaches its optimal operating capacity when inputs, labour and/or production factors are used to the maximum to ensure the maximum output. When a new business is established, it seldom functions at full capacity from the start. There are therefore usually fewer orders or a lesser demand than can be provided. The business possibly starts below or at the break-even point, with the prospect of obtaining more business in time to function optimally. This will ensure increased profits. Remember, however, that the availability of specific equipment and labour is crucial to the production of a particular quantity of products.

There may come a time when demand exceeds maximum output and additional costs may have to be incurred to meet this demand. It may not be possible to make provision for only one increase in demand. Suppose the demand for a product rises by 100 units. The equipment for manufacturing the 100 additional units costs R12 000. This expenditure, however, causes the production capacity to be raised and an additional 800 units can be manufactured. At this point, a new break-even point must be calculated to determine whether it is worthwhile raising the production capacity. If the continued demand does not justify the purchase of additional equipment, other methods must be found to increase outputs. Examples are:

- overtime
- producing during quiet periods for stock build-up
- contracting out certain functions or processes
- contracting out for the manufacture of specific quantities of products
- hiring equipment
- appointing temporary labour and/or labour on contract.

Thus you must ensure that the possible expansion of your business results in a real increase in income. The expense must not exceed the expected income as a result of the expansion of capacity. In certain cases, such as when a constant increase in demand is expected, higher expenses than income are acceptable at first. In such a case, it is important that meaningful forecasts and planning takes place to ensure profitability, in the long term.

Another managerial responsibility is to draw up well-considered contracts between relevant parties. These include contracts between the business and:

- employees
- landlords
- clients.

Clear and unambiguous contracts avoid financial, personal and even legal conflicts.

6.8 Summary

When a new business is established, the setting-up and establishment factors are not equal for all businesses. The entrepreneur has to determine which factors are critical for success. When planning the business he or she must concentrate on these factors. Remember that the emphasis of the business often shifts and that growth makes different demands on the entrepreneur. A business that at first had few or no staff will have to appoint more staff eventually, or an entrepreneur who does his or her own marketing at first will later make use of a marketing specialist. The entrepreneur must therefore note the critical success factors in the setting-up stage, but be aware of the fact that the situation is not static. Change comes rapidly and it is important to make provision for it timeously to ensure competitiveness.

Self-evaluation questions

1. List the most suitable form of business for the business you are planning and give three reasons for your choice.
2. Briefly describe your planned business and indicate which legal registrations and requirements for licensing are applicable.
3. Considering the same business you described in your answer to Question 2, list the most important factors in the choice of a location and indicate why each plays a role.
4. To which initial marketing elements of the business functions must attention be given in the setting-up stage of your proposed business (as described in your answer to Question 2)?
5. How will you manage each business function in the setting-up stage you described in the answer to Question 2?

References and further reading

Companies Regulations, 2011. Government Gazette. http://www.dti.gov.za/ccrd/regulations.pdf (accessed 29 April 2011).

Consumer Protection Act No. 68 of 2008. 2011. Government Gazette. 1 April. http://www.dti.gov.za/ccrd/notice_threshold.pdf (accessed 29 April 2011).

Department of Labour. 1995. Labour Relations Act No. 66 of 1995. *Government Gazette*, vol. 366, no. 16861. Cape Town. 13 December 1995. http://www.polity.org/govdocs/legislation/1995/ act95-066.html (accessed 30 August 2011).

Department of Labour. 1997. Basic Conditions of Employment Act No. 75 of 1997. http://www.polity.org/govdocs/regulations/1998/reg98-1438.html (accessed 30 August 2011).

Department of Labour. 1998. Employment Equity Act No. 55 of 1998. *Government Gazette*, vol. 400, no. 1323. Cape Town. 19 October 1998.

Department of Labour. 2003. Broad Based Black Economic Empowerment Act 53 of 2003. http://www.polity.org/govdocs/regulations/2003/act (accessed 30 August 2011).

BUSINESS PLAN FOR:

January 2012

Business Plan Copy Number 1

**This document contains confidential and proprietary information
belonging exclusively to Ntombi's Milk Market CC.**

Ntombi Mashaba
Chief Executive Officer
Mamelodi East x4435
Gauteng
Tel: 098 998 7894
Email: ntombi@milk.co.za
Web: www.ntombimilkmarket.co.za

This is a business plan. It does not imply an offering of securities.

Confidentiality Agreement

Date: 2012/03/01

The Investor acknowledges that Ms Ntombi Mashaba has furnished to the Investor parties certain proprietary data ('Confidential Information') relating to the business affairs and operations of Ntombi's Milk Market CC for study and evaluation by Investor for possible investment.

It is acknowledged by the Investor that the information provided by Ms Ntombi Mashaba is confidential; therefore, the Investor agrees not to disclose it and not to disclose that any discussions or contracts with Ms Ntombi Mashaba have occurred or are intended, other than as provided for in the following paragraph.

It is acknowledged by the Investor that information to be furnished is in all respects confidential in nature, other than information which is in the public domain through other means, and that any disclosure or use of same by the Investor, except as provided in this agreement, may cause serious harm or damage to Ntombi's Milk Market CC, and its owners and officers. Therefore, the Investor agrees that the parties will not use the information furnished for any purpose other than as stated above, and agrees that the parties will not either directly or indirectly by agent, employee or representative, disclose this information, either in whole or in part, to any third party; provided, however that (a) information furnished may be disclosed only to those directors, officers and employees of Investor and to Investor's advisors of their representatives who need such information for the purpose of evaluating any possible transaction (it being understood that those directors, officers, employees, advisors and representatives shall be informed by the Investor of the confidential nature of such information and shall be directed by the Investor to treat such information confidentially), and (b) any disclosure of information may be made to which the Investor consents in writing. At the close of negotiations, Investor will return to Ntombi's Milk Market CC all records, reports, documents, and memoranda furnished and will not make or retain any copy thereof.

_____ **2012/03/01**

Signature of Investor Date

Mr Rupert Buys
Name

Table of Contents

1. Executive summary

Ntombi Mashaba established Ntombi's Milk Market in 1997 in the eastern Mamelodi area, Gauteng. Her humble beginning as an entrepreneur entailed buying milk from a dairy farmer close to this area and reselling it to her neighbours, from her 20m² bedroom. The need for different quantities of fresh milk, available on a daily basis, evolved into the establishment of a small retail outlet and later developed into the 200m² Mamelodi Dairy Market, a well-known landmark in this region. Fresh milk is sold in different quantities according to the specific needs of the customer.

Ntombi also identified and exploited the opportunity to make cheese and yogurt as derivative products of milk. This business unit operates from a factory in Watloo, Pretoria. It follows a focused and differentiated strategy in providing customised products to delicatessen and home industries in the broader Tshwane metropolitan area.

The business intends to increase its turnover to R4.5 million in 2013 with specific growth strategies in place, as explained in more detail in the business plan. The gross profit margin equals approximately 60%.

The purpose of this plan is primarily to serve as a planning instrument and will be adapted to the needs of an investor in order to finance some of the medium-term growth strategies, for example the purchase of a dairy farm.

2. Business description

2.1 General description of the business

Ntombi's Milk Market is a close corporation (CC) established in 1997. It initially operated as a milk re-seller in the Mamelodi area. The business grew organically and diversified to include different milk formats (in terms of packaging), yogurt and cheese. The current market expanded from the Lusaka area in the eastern Mamelodi area, to include up-market delicatessens and home industries in the entire Tshwane metropolitan area.

Ntombi's Milk Market's distribution structure is channelled as follows:

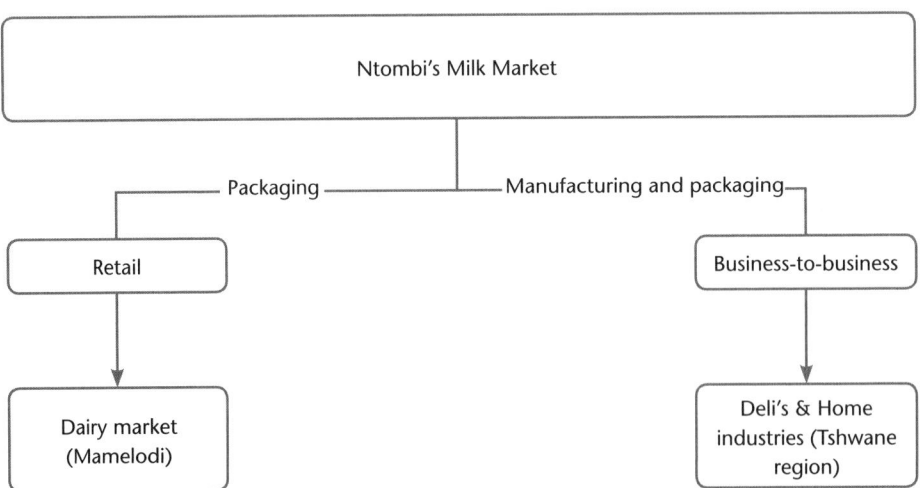

Ntombi's Milk Market operates from a medium-sized manufacturing unit in the industrial area of Watloo, Silverton (Pretoria) where all the fresh milk is received and either repackaged in smaller units (500 ml, 1 l or 2 l) or transformed into yogurt and cheese products.

Ntombi's Milk Market owns a dairy market with an approximate size of 200m², which was opened in 2001 in the eastern Mamelodi area. This retail outlet only sells fresh milk to residents in the area in either bulk or smaller units.

The business-to-business leg of the business entails offering yogurt and cheese products to five delicatessens and 15 home industries in the broader Tshwane metropolitan area. Ntombi's Milk Market intends to expand this offering to the northern parts of Johannesburg in the near future.

2.2   Industry background

The dairy branch of industry has the following characteristics relevant to the retail end:

* a growing demand for healthy dairy-related products (eg no-fat and low-fat products)
* a low-profit margin for the producer
* a decline in the number of producers of fresh milk
* an increase in the cost of transport for perishable products
* a big increase in consumer spending on retail goods
* a big demand for specialised dairy products (eg cheese).

2.3   Primary goals of the business

Ntombi's Milk Market has the following objectives:

Short term (2012–2013):

* To increase its overall turnover to R4 437 245.
* To obtain two contracts for delivery of cheese and yogurt in the Northern Johannesburg region.
* To buy another truck for self delivery.
* To appoint a general manager at the factory.
* To identify potential dairy farms for purchase.

Medium term (2014–2016):

* To increase overall turnover to R6 million per annum.
* To obtain seven contracts for the delivery of cheese and yogurt in the Northern Johannesburg region.
* To establish a delivery network of at least four trucks.
* To expand the factory layout to 1000m².
* To purchase a dairy farm (backward integration) close to the Mamelodi Dairy Market as a sole self supplier.

Long term (2017–2021):

* To increase turnover to R10 million per annum.
* To become the leading BEE milk and related product provider in Gauteng.

2.4 Uniqueness of the product/service

Ntombi's Milk Market strives to produce all its products based on above-average quality standards. Ntombi's offers the following unique services:

Mamelodi Dairy Market:

- offers fresh milk six days a week from 07h00 to 18h00, thereby enabling working parents and households to buy milk before and/or after work.
- allows customers to use and re-use their own containers of any size.
- provides adequate parking and enough attendants at the cash registers to serve and limit long queues.
- provides information booklets on the health aspects of dairy products and basic recipes.
- maintains a loyal customer base.
- has a low price strategy, especially for customers with own containers.

Business-to-business:

- offers custom-made yogurt and cheese products with unique characteristics and shapes.
- ensures a continuous supply based on customer demand.
- provides fresh delivery.
- maintains good relationships with customers.

3. Marketing plan

3.1 Marketing research and analysis

A survey was conducted by a private research entity concerning the need for dairy products in the Mamelodi area. The full report is attached in the Appendix. The results showed that there is a huge need for fresh milk, particularly milk at a better price than available at the Spaza outlets in the area. The quality of the milk is also of great concern.

3.2 Target market

The market for Ntombi's Milk Market is segmented and forms two basic target markets. The first pertains to the Mamelodi Dairy Market. The characteristics of this target market are as follows:

- households within a 5 km radius of the outlet, living in the eastern side of Mamelodi
- households with an average size of 5 individuals
- households with an income between R1 500 and R5 000 per month
- households that buy milk twice a week (with an average of 2 litres per purchase).

Women form the primary purchaser of fresh milk in this region.

The business-to-business leg of the business has the following market:

- delicatessens in the Tshwane metropolitan area, focusing on the top end of the market (high income), selling 'homemade' yogurt and cheese
- home industries in the Tshwane metropolitan area, focusing on the top end of the market (high income), selling 'homemade' yogurt and cheese.

3.3 Market size and market share

The current market size for both these target markets is:

- Mamelodi Dairy Market: 120 000 households of which it is believed Ntombi's Milk Market has captured 40%.
- Business-to-business: There are 35 delicatessens and home industries in the Tshwane area, of which Ntombi's Milk Market is believed to have captured 57%.

3.4 Competition

Ntombi's Milk Market operates in a highly competitive market environment and competes with the following (a detailed competitive analysis is available on request):

- Mamelodi Dairy Market:
  a. Spaza shops (eight in the immediate market environment).
  b. Checkers, approximately 7 km from the outlet.
  c. Outside the area—indirect competition (households buying milk on their way home from work).

- Business-to-business:
  a. Large suppliers selling bulk units (eg Makro and Trade Centre), although not the same specialised products.
  b. Dairy farms surrounding the Tshwane area with more or less the same product types.
  c. Importing companies that obtain specialised cheeses from the Netherlands and Switzerland as well as other regions in South Africa (although not as price effective).

3.5 Marketing strategy

Product strategy

The following product mix is offered:

- Mamelodi Dairy Market:

Fresh milk in containers (full cream):
500 ml containers (plastic)
1 litre containers (plastic)
2 litre containers (plastic)

Fresh milk in own containers (full cream):
Any volumes between 500 ml and 5 litres

- Business-to-business

Yogurt:
300 ml plastic container, flavoured: strawberry, vanilla, chocolate
1 litre plastic container, flavoured: strawberry, vanilla, chocolate
5 litre plastic container, unflavoured

Cheese:
200 g to 2 kg cheddar
500 g to 2 kg feta
200 g to 2 kg gouda

Pricing strategy

The following pricing applies:

- Mamelodi Dairy Market:

Fresh milk in containers (full cream):	Price (R) per unit:
500 ml containers (plastic)	5,00
1 litre containers (plastic)	7,00
2 litre containers (plastic)	10,00

Fresh milk in own containers (full cream):	Price (R) per unit:
Any volume between 500 ml and 5 litres	6,00/litre

- Business-to-business:

Yogurt:	Price (R) per unit:
300 ml plastic container, flavoured: strawberry, vanilla, chocolate	3,00
1 litre plastic container, flavoured: strawberry, vanilla, chocolate	11,00
5 litre plastic container, unflavoured	40,00

Cheese:	Price (R) per unit:
200 g to 2 kg cheddar	80,00/kg
500 g to 2 kg feta	110,00/kg
200 g to 2 kg gouda	85,00/kg

Promotion strategy

Ntombi's Milk Market follows the following promotion strategy with regard to its product range:

- Mamelodi Dairy Market:
  Currently the most effective medium of promotion for this leg of the business is by word of mouth. The Mamelodi Dairy Market is known for its quick and effective service, the quality as well as the availability of fresh milk. Ntombi Mashaba realised that community involvement also plays an enormous role in promoting the business. She developed a very neat soccer field at the back of the outlet and invests in experienced coaches for the development of young players. Apart from the latter, a 2 m x 3 m billboard serves as the main advertising medium. This board indicates all the specials that run every fortnight

- Business-to-business:
  The promotion strategy for this business unit is twofold. Direct marketing to all the Delis and Home industries seems to be the most effective medium to date. Ntombi attends to this medium herself. Each and every retail outlet is visited on a monthly

basis (in terms of the retainer customers) and she endeavours to see at least one new customer per month. The entire product line is shown and even tasted and afterwards adapted to the exact needs of customers (retailers). The second format of promotion is the attendance of at least three trade shows per annum. Ntombi links her promotion strategy with the capacity of her factory and tries not to oversell.

Distribution strategy

Ntombi's Milk Market obtains all its milk from a very reliable dairy farmer close to the small town Cullinan. This farm is approximately 8 km from the Mamelodi Dairy Market and 14 km from the factory in Watloo. The short distance from the supplier forms part of the core competence of this business due to the increasingly high cost of the transport of perishable products. The farmer delivers directly to the dairy market at a cost of R10/km. Ntombi decided to buy a cooler truck for transferring the milk to the factory in Watloo. This truck is also easily adapted to a delivery vehicle for the business-to-business unit. The milk delivery to the factory takes place on a daily basis and deliveries to the retail customers once a week (with an increase during high season).

4. Location

Both the dairy market and factory are located, firstly, close to the supplier (as indicated in the Marketing plan) and, secondly, close to its consecutive groups of customers. The expansion ability on both these sites is possible within the long-term objectives of the business. Ntombi employs only people from the immediate community and provides them with training as needed. Employees therefore don't have to travel that far to work and the skills development will enhance the community at large.

5. Management plan

Ntombi's Milk Market has reached a point where a professional management team should replace the over-emphasised role of the entrepreneur and founder (Ntombi Mashaba). Ntombi currently works seven days a week for approximately 12 hours a day.

5.1 Organisational structure

The business therefore plans to re-organise its structure in order to enable Ntombi to spend more time on strategic issues, compulsory for effective growth. The curriculum vitae of each staff member will be provided upon request. The following organisation structure is to be implemented in the short term:

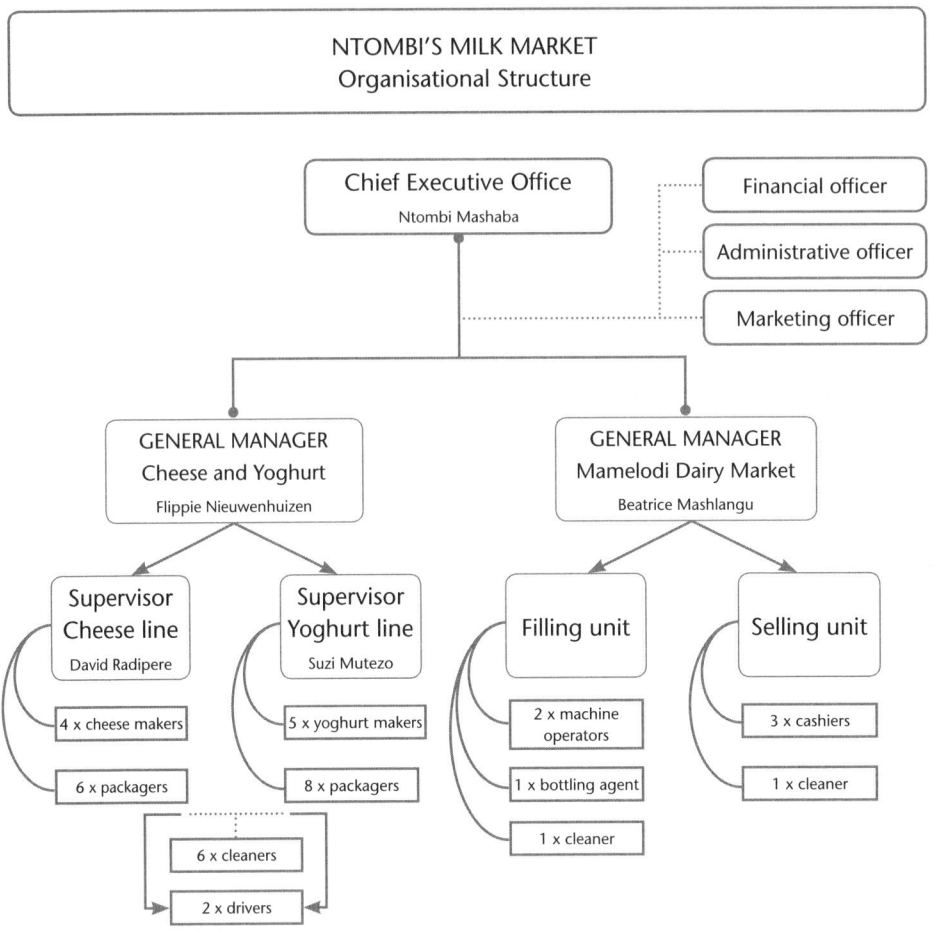

5.2 Human resources plan

Ntombi formulated a job description and job specification for each and every position created in the organisational structure. She is also a firm believer in human development and plans to enrol most of the staff in applicable learnerships in their relevant fields. Ntombi's Milk Market also complies with the following legislation:

- Labour relations Act No. 66 of 1995
- Basic Conditions of Employment Act No. 75 of 1997
- Employment Equity Act No. 55 of 1998
- Skills Development Act No. 97 of 1998
- Skills Development Levies Act No. 9 of 1999.

5.2.1 Ownership structure

Ntombi Mashaba is currently the only member in Ntombi Milk Market CC (Ck 1997/446665/23) and operates with a 100% BEE status. Ntombi intends to sell a 20% membership in her business in order to finance her growth strategies. Another 6% will be distributed to staff members, based on an incentive scheme (to be developed).

6. Financial plan

NTOMBI'S MILK MARKET			
PROJECTED BALANCE SHEET			
	Realistic local scenario projections		
	2012	**2013**	**2014**
CAPITAL EMPLOYED			
Member equity	200 000	200 000	200 000
Retained earnings	500 000	500 000	500 000
Member shareholding	700 000	700 000	700 000
	425 747	340 405	242 317
Loan	**1 125 747**	**1 040 405**	**942 317**
EMPLOYMENT OF CAPITAL			
TOTAL ASSETS	**1 535 956**	**1 692 297**	**1 615 124**
FIXED ASSETS	881 063	881 063	881 063
Buildings, furniture and equipment	804 738	804 738	804 738
Setup Cost	76 325	76 325	76 325
CURRENT ASSETS	654 893	811 234	734 061
Initial operating capital	81 937	81 937	81 937
Bank	572 956	729 297	652 124
Minus:			
CURRENT LIABILITIES			
Dividends payable	302 525	536 852	567 079
Receiver Revenue	107 684	115 040	121 517
	410 209	651 892	688 596
	1 125 747	**1 040 405**	**926 528**

NTOMBI'S MILK MARKET		Realistic scenario projections	
Projected Income Statement			

	Projections			Total
	2012	2013	2014	Total
INCOME:	3 400 000	3 604 000	3 892 320	10 896 320
Cost of Sales	1 326 000	1 405 560	1 518 005	4 249 565
Gross profit	2 074 000	2 198 440	2 374 315	6 646 755
Gross profit %	61%	61%	61%	61%
Operations expenditure	1 290 752	1 377 243	1 522 682	4 190 677
Advertising and promotions	68 000	72 080	77 846	217 926
Bank services charges	7 820	8 289	8 952	25 062
Credit card charges	38 760	41 086	44 372	124 218
Cleaning Materials	5 100	5 406	5 838	16 344
First Aid	1 020	1 081	1 168	3 269
Insurance	10 200	10 812	11 677	32 689
Insurance Vehicles	0	0	0	0
Laundry	2 040	2 162	2 335	6 538
Licenses and Permits	3 740	3 964	4 282	11 986
Medical Aid	0	0	0	0
Motor expense				0
Petrol	1 000	0	24 000	25 000
Motor expense - other	0	0	5 702	5 702
Postage and Delivery	340	360	389	1 090
Printing and reproduction	1 700	1 802	1 946	5 448
Professional fees				0
Accounting	7 820	8 289	8 952	25 062
Consulting	3 400	3 604	3 892	10 896
Protective clothing	4 760	5 046	5 449	15 255
Refreshments	0	0	0	0
Refuse removal	3 400	3 604	3 892	10 896
Rent (fixed)	252 632	277 895	305 684	836 211
Repairs				0
Building repairs	3 060	3 244	3 503	9 807
Computer repairs	1 020	1 081	1 168	3 269
Equipment repairs	11 560	12 254	13 234	37 047
Rates and Taxes	3 060	3 244	3 503	9 807
Security	4 080	4 325	4 671	13 076
Stationary and printing	3 740	3 964	4 282	11 986
Subscpritions	680	721	778	2 179
Telephone				0
Fax	1 700	1 802	1 946	5 448
Mobile	0	0	0	0
Telephone - other	3 400	3 604	3 892	10 896
Replacement of machinery	17 000	18 020	19 462	54 482
Travel and entertainment				0
Entertainment	0	0	0	0
Travel	0	0	0	0
Travel and entertainment - other	0	0	0	0
Utilities				0
Water	5 100	5 406	5 838	16 344
Gas and Electric	28 220	29 913	32 306	90 439
Uniforms	3 740	3 964	4 282	11 986
Unemployment insurance fund	3 400	3 604	3 892	10 896
Workman's compensation fund	2 380	2 523	2 725	7 627
Installment vehicle	66 081	70 046	75 649	211 776
Gifts and donations	3 400	3 604	3 892	10 896
Member Salary - A	51 000	54 060	58 385	163 445
Member salary - B	51 000	54 060	58 385	163 445
RSC Levy	6 800	7 208	7 785	21 793
Salaries	258 400	273 904	295 816	828 120
Wages	336 600	356 796	385 340	1 078 736
Staff meals	10 200	10 812	11 677	32 689
Skills Development	3 400	3 604	3 892	10 896
Total operating expenditure	1 290 752	1 377 243 0	1 522 682	4 190 677
Nett Profit before financial-exp	783 248	821 197	851 633	2 456 078
Nett Profit BIT %	23%	23%	22%	23%
Interest expense	65 355	54 266	41 520	
Nett Profit before tax	717 893	766 931	810 113	2 294 937
Nett Profit %	21%	21%	21%	21%
Tax @ 30%	215 368	230 079	243 034	688 481
Nett Profit after tax	502 525	536 852	567 079	1 606 456
Nett Profit %	15%	15%	15%	14.74%
Acc profit(loss) at start period	0	200 000	200 000	
Dividends paid	302 525	536 852	567 079	1 406 456
Acc profit(loss) at end of period	200 000	200 000	200 000	200 000

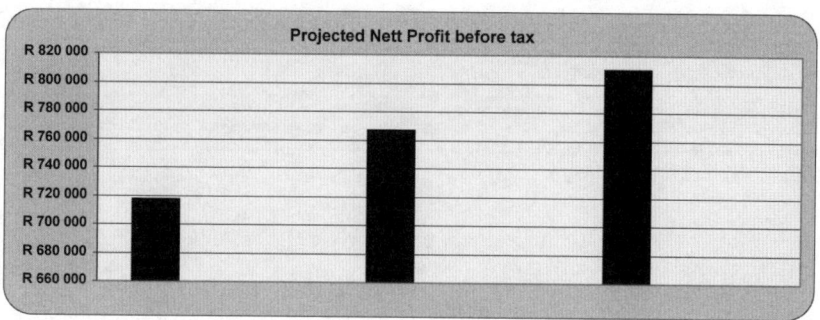

Cash Flow Forecast May 2012 to April 2013

			May-12	Jun-12	Jul-12	Aug-12	Sep-12	Oct-12
							NTOMBI'S MILK MARKET	CASHFLOW FORECAST
Percentage of total sales per month		1	0.0736	0.0736	0.0784	0.0784	0.0833	0.0833
Sales		3 876 000	285 274	285 274	303 878	303 878	322 871	322 871
INCOME:								
Sales		3 876 000	285 274	285 274	303 878	303 878	322 871	322 871
Total Income:			**285 274**	**285 274**	**303 878**	**303 878**	**322 871**	**322 871**
COST OF SALES:								
Cost of sales		39%	111 257	111 257	118 513	118 513	125 920	125 920
Total Cost of Sales:			**111 257**	**111 257**	**118 513**	**118 513**	**125 920**	**125 920**
	Gross profit		174 017	174 017	185 366	185 366	196 951	196 951
	Gross profit %		61%	61%	61%	61%	61%	61%
OPERATING EXPENDITURE								
Advertising and promotions		2.00%	5 705	5 705	6 078	6 078	6 457	6 457
Bank services charges		0.23%	656	656	699	699	743	743
Credit card charges		1.14%	3 252	3 252	3 464	3 464	3 681	3 681
Cleaning Materials		0.15%	428	428	456	456	484	484
First Aid		0.03%	86	86	91	91	97	97
Insurance		0.30%	856	856	912	912	969	969
Insurance Vehicles		0.00%	0	0	0	0	0	0
Laundry		0.06%	171	171	182	182	194	194
Licenses and Permits		0.11%	314	314	334	334	355	355
Medical Aid		0.00%	0	0	0	0	0	0
Motor expense								
Petrol		0.00%	1 000	0	0	0	0	0
Motor expense - other		0.00%	0	0	0	0	0	0
Postage and Delivery		0.01%	29	29	30	30	32	32
Printing and reproduction		0.05%	143	143	152	152	161	161
Professional fees								
Accounting		0.23%	656	656	699	699	743	743
Consulting		0.10%	285	285	304	304	323	323
Protective clothing		0.14%	399	399	425	425	452	452
Refreshments		0.00%	0	0	0	0	0	0
Refuse removal		0.10%	285	285	304	304	323	323
Rent (fixed)		24 000	24 000	24 000	24 000	24 000	24 000	24 000
Repairs								
Building repairs		0.09%	257	257	273	273	291	291
Computer repairs		0.03%	86	86	91	91	97	97
Equipment repairs		0.34%	970	970	1 033	1 033	1 098	1 098
Rates and Taxes		0.09%	257	257	273	273	291	291
Security		0.12%	342	342	365	365	387	387
Stationary and printing		0.11%	314	314	334	334	355	355
Subscriptions		0.02%	57	57	61	61	65	65
Telephone								
Fax		0.05%	143	143	152	152	161	161
Mobile		0.00%	0	0	0	0	0	0
Telephone - other		0.10%	285	285	304	304	323	323
Replacement of machinery		0.50%	1 426	1 426	1 519	1 519	1 614	1 614
Travel and entertainment								
Entertainment		0.00%	0	0	0	0	0	0
Travel		0.00%	0	0	0	0	0	0
Travel and entertainment - other		0.00%	0	0	0	0	0	0
Utilities								
Water		0.15%	428	428	456	456	484	484
Gas and Electric		0.83%	2 368	2 368	2 522	2 522	2 680	2 680
Uniforms		0.11%	314	314	334	334	355	355
Unemployment insurance fund		0.09%	250	250	267	267	283	283
Workman's compensation fund		0.06%	175	175	187	187	198	198
Installment vehicle		1.71%	4 864	4 864	5 181	5 181	5 505	5 505
Gifts and donations		0.09%	250	250	267	267	283	283
Member Salary - A		1.32%	3 754	3 754	3 998	3 998	4 248	4 248
Member salary - B		1.32%	3 754	3 754	3 998	3 998	4 248	4 248
RSC Levy		0.18%	500	500	533	533	566	566
Salaries		6.67%	19 018	19 018	20 259	20 259	21 525	21 525
Wages		8.68%	24 774	24 774	26 389	26 389	28 039	28 039
Staff meals		0.26%	751	751	800	800	850	850
Skills Development		0.09%	250	250	267	267	283	283
Total operations expenditure (incl VAT):			*103 851*	*102 851*	*107 993*	*107 993*	*113 243*	*113 243*
VAT at 14%				-31 808		-34 267		-36 777
Total net profit (after accounting for VAT):			*70 166*	*39 357*	*77 372*	*43 105*	*83 708*	*46 931*
FINANCING EXPENSES								
Capital repayment		500 000	5 801	5 868	5 937	6 006	6 076	6 147
Interest		14%	5 833	5 766	5 697	5 628	5 558	5 487
Total cash flow after financing repayments:			*58 532*	*27 723*	*65 738*	*31 471*	*72 074*	*35 297*
Retained cash per month	Nett Profit		58 532	27 723	65 738	31 471	72 074	35 297
	Nett Profit %		21%	10%	22%	10%	22%	11%
Dividend payment								
Tax payment								
Cashflow position			95 532	123 255	188 994	220 465	292 539	327 836
	R 37 000.00	Start fin year						

138

MAY 2012 TO APR 2013	Realistic scenario					
Nov-12	**Dec-12**	**Jan-13**	**Feb-13**	**Mar-13**	**Apr-13**	**TOTAL**
0.0882	0.0882	0.0882	0.0882	0.0883	0.0883	1
341 863	341 863	341 863	341 863	342 251	342 251	3 876 000
341 863	341 863	341 863	341 863	342 251	342 251	3 876 000
341 863	**341 863**	**341 863**	**341 863**	**342 251**	**342 251**	3 876 000
133 327	133 327	133 327	133 327	133 478	133 478	1 511 640
133 327	**133 327**	**133 327**	**133 327**	**133 478**	**133 478**	1 511 640
208 537	208 537	208 537	208 537	208 773	208 773	2 364 360
61%	**61%**	**61%**	**61%**	**61%**	**61%**	**61%**
6 837	6 837	6 837	6 837	6 845	6 845	77 520
786	786	786	786	787	787	8 915
3 897	3 897	3 897	3 897	3 902	3 902	44 186
513	513	513	513	513	513	5 814
103	103	103	103	103	103	1 163
1 026	1 026	1 026	1 026	1 027	1 027	11 628
0	0	0	0	0	0	0
205	205	205	205	205	205	2 326
376	376	376	376	376	376	4 264
0	0	0	0	0	0	0
0	0	0	0	0	0	1 000
0	0	0	0	0	0	0
34	34	34	34	34	34	388
171	171	171	171	171	171	1 938
786	786	786	786	787	787	8 915
342	342	342	342	342	342	3 876
479	479	479	479	479	479	5 426
0	0	0	0	0	0	0
342	342	342	342	342	342	3 876
24 000	24 000	24 000	24 000	24 000	24 000	288 000
308	308	308	308	308	308	3 488
103	103	103	103	103	103	1 163
1 162	1 162	1 162	1 162	1 164	1 164	13 178
308	308	308	308	308	308	3 488
410	410	410	410	411	411	4 651
376	376	376	376	376	376	4 264
68	68	68	68	68	68	775
171	171	171	171	171	171	1 938
0	0	0	0	0	0	0
342	342	342	342	342	342	3 876
1 709	1 709	1 709	1 709	1 711	1 711	19 380
0	0	0	0	0	0	0
0	0	0	0	0	0	0
0	0	0	0	0	0	0
513	513	513	513	513	513	5 814
2 837	2 837	2 837	2 837	2 841	2 841	32 171
376	376	376	376	376	376	4 264
300	300	300	300	300	300	3 400
210	210	210	210	210	210	2 380
5 828	5 828	5 828	5 828	5 835	5 835	66 081
300	300	300	300	300	300	3 400
4 498	4 498	4 498	4 498	4 503	4 503	51 000
4 498	4 498	4 498	4 498	4 503	4 503	51 000
600	600	600	600	600	600	6 800
22 791	22 791	22 791	22 791	22 817	22 817	258 400
29 688	29 688	29 688	29 688	29 722	29 722	336 600
900	900	900	900	901	901	10 200
300	300	300	300	300	300	3 400
118 493	*118 493*	*118 493*	*118 493*	*118 600*	*118 600*	*1 360 345*
	-39 288		-39 288		-39 339	-220 767
90 044	*50 756*	*90 044*	*50 756*	*90 173*	*50 834*	*783 248*
6 219	6 291	6 365	6 439	6 514	6 590	74 253
5 415	5 343	5 269	5 195	5 120	5 044	65 355
78 410	*39 122*	*78 410*	*39 122*	*78 539*	*39 200*	*643 640*
78 410	39 122	78 410	39 122	78 539	39 200	643 640
23%	11%	23%	11%	23%	11%	17%
						0
107 684						107 684
298 562	337 684	416 094	455 216	533 755	572 956	572 956

(100.0% / 100%)

			NTOMBI'S MILK MARKET		CASHFLOW FORECAST		
Annual CPIX increase factor:	1.060	**May-12**	**Jun-12**	**Jul-12**	**Aug-12**	**Sep-12**	**Oct-12**
Percentage of total sales per month	1	0.0736	0.0736	0.0784	0.0784	0.0833	0.0833
Sales	4 108 560	302 390	302 390	322 111	322 111	342 243	342 243
INCOME:							
Sales	4 108 560	302 390	302 390	322 111	322 111	342 243	342 243
Total Income:		**302 390**	**302 390**	**322 111**	**322 111**	**342 243**	**342 243**
COST OF SALES:							
Cost of sales	39%	117 932	117 932	125 623	125 623	133 475	133 475
Total Cost Sales		**117 932**	**117 932**	**125 623**	**125 623**	**133 475**	**133 475**
Gross profit		184 458	184 458	196 488	196 488	208 768	208 768
Gross profit %		61%	61%	61%	61%	61%	61%
OPERATING EXPENDITURE							
Advertising and promotions	2.00%	6 048	6 048	6 442	6 442	6 845	6 845
Bank services charges	0.23%	695	695	741	741	787	787
Credit card charges	1.14%	3 447	3 447	3 672	3 672	3 902	3 902
Cleaning Materials	0.15%	454	454	483	483	513	513
First Aid	0.03%	91	91	97	97	103	103
Insurance	0.30%	907	907	966	966	1 027	1 027
Insurance Vehicles	0.00%	0	0	0	0	0	0
Laundry	0.06%	181	181	193	193	205	205
Licenses and Permits	0.11%	333	333	354	354	376	376
Medical Aid	0.00%	0	0	0	0	0	0
Motor expense							
Petrol	0.00%	0	0	0	0	0	0
Motor expense - other	0.00%	0	0	0	0	0	0
Postage and Delivery	0.01%	30	30	32	32	34	34
Printing and reproduction	0.05%	151	151	161	161	171	171
Professional fees							
Accounting	0.23%	695	695	741	741	787	787
Consulting	0.10%	302	302	322	322	342	342
Protective clothing	0.14%	423	423	451	451	479	479
Refreshments	0.00%	0	0	0	0	0	0
Refuse removal	0.10%	302	302	322	322	342	342
Rent (fixed)	26 400	26 400	26 400	26 400	26 400	26 400	26 400
Repairs							
Building repairs	0.09%	272	272	290	290	308	308
Computer repairs	0.03%	91	91	97	97	103	103
Equipment repairs	0.34%	1 028	1 028	1 095	1 095	1 164	1 164
Rates and Taxes	0.09%	272	272	290	290	308	308
Security	0.12%	363	363	387	387	411	411
Stationary and printing	0.11%	333	333	354	354	376	376
Subscriptions	0.02%	60	60	64	64	68	68
Telephone							
Fax	0.05%	151	151	161	161	171	171
Mobile	0.00%	0	0	0	0	0	0
Telephone - other	0.10%	302	302	322	322	342	342
Replacement of machinery	0.50%	1 512	1 512	1 611	1 611	1 711	1 711
Travel and entertainment							
Entertainment	0.00%	0	0	0	0	0	0
Travel	0.00%	0	0	0	0	0	0
Travel and entertainment - other	0.00%	0	0	0	0	0	0
Utilities							
Water	0.15%	454	454	483	483	513	513
Gas and Electric	0.83%	2 510	2 510	2 674	2 674	2 841	2 841
Uniforms	0.11%	333	333	354	354	376	376
Unemployment insurance fund	0.09%	265	265	283	283	300	300
Workman's compensation fund	0.06%	186	186	198	198	210	210
Installment vehicle	1.71%	5 155	5 155	5 492	5 492	5 835	5 835
Gifts and donations	0.09%	265	265	283	283	300	300
Member Salary - A	1.32%	3 979	3 979	4 238	4 238	4 503	4 503
Member salary - B	1.32%	3 979	3 979	4 238	4 238	4 503	4 503
RSC Levy	0.18%	531	531	565	565	600	600
Salaries	6.67%	20 159	20 159	21 474	21 474	22 816	22 816
Wages	8.68%	26 260	26 260	27 973	27 973	29 721	29 721
Staff meals	0.26%	796	796	848	848	901	901
Skills Development	0.09%	265	265	283	283	300	300
Total operations expenditure (incl VAT):		**109 982**	**109 982**	**115 433**	**115 433**	**120 998**	**120 998**
VAT at 14%		-33 481		-36 088			-38 748
Total net profit (after accounting for VAT):		*74 476*	*40 995*	*81 055*	*44 967*	*87 771*	*49 022*
FINANCING EXPENSES							
Capital repayment		**6 667**	**6 745**	**6 823**	**6 903**	**6 984**	**7 065**
Interest		**4 967**	**4 889**	**4 811**	**4 731**	**4 650**	**4 569**
Total cash flow after financing repayments:		*62 842*	*29 361*	*69 421*	*33 333*	*76 137*	*37 388*
Retained cash per month	Nett Profit	62 842	29 361	69 421	33 333	76 137	37 388
	Nett Profit %	21%	10%	22%	10%	22%	11%
Dividend payment		25 210	25 210	25 210	25 210	25 210	25 210
Tax payment		107 684					
Cashflow position		502 903	507 054	551 264	559 387	610 313	622 491
	R 572 955.76	Start fin year					

MAY 2012 TO APR 2013		Realistic scenario					
Nov-12	Dec-12	Jan-13	Feb-13	Mar-13	Apr-13	TOTAL	
0.0882	0.0882	0.0882	0.0882	0.0883	0.0883	1	0
362 375	362 375	362 375	362 375	362 786	362 786	4 108 560	
362 375	362 375	362 375	362 375	362 786	362 786	4 108 560	100.0%
362 375	**362 375**	**362 375**	**362 375**	**362 786**	**362 786**	4 108 560	**100%**
141 326	141 326	141 326	141 326	141 486	141 486	1 602 338	
141 326	**141 326**	**141 326**	**141 326**	**141 486**	**141 486**	1 602 338	
221 049	**221 049**	**221 049**	**221 049**	**221 299**	**221 299**	**2 506 222**	
61%	61%	61%	61%	61%	61%	61%	
7 247	7 247	7 247	7 247	7 256	7 256	82 171	
833	833	833	833	834	834	9 450	
4 131	4 131	4 131	4 131	4 136	4 136	46 838	
544	544	544	544	544	544	6 163	
109	109	109	109	109	109	1 233	
1 087	1 087	1 087	1 087	1 088	1 088	12 326	
0	0	0	0	0	0	0	
217	217	217	217	218	218	2 465	
399	399	399	399	399	399	4 519	
0	0	0	0	0	0	0	
0	0	0	0	0	0	0	
0	0	0	0	0	0	0	
36	36	36	36	36	36	411	
181	181	181	181	181	181	2 054	
833	833	833	833	834	834	9 450	
362	362	362	362	363	363	4 109	
507	507	507	507	508	508	5 752	
0	0	0	0	0	0	0	
362	362	362	362	363	363	4 109	
26 400	26 400	26 400	26 400	26 400	26 400	316 800	
326	326	326	326	327	327	3 698	
109	109	109	109	109	109	1 233	
1 232	1 232	1 232	1 232	1 233	1 233	13 969	
326	326	326	326	327	327	3 698	
435	435	435	435	435	435	4 930	
399	399	399	399	399	399	4 519	
72	72	72	72	73	73	822	
							0
181	181	181	181	181	181	2 054	
0	0	0	0	0	0	0	
362	362	362	362	363	363	4 109	
1 812	1 812	1 812	1 812	1 814	1 814	20 543	
							0
0	0	0	0	0	0	0	
0	0	0	0	0	0	0	
0	0	0	0	0	0	0	
							0
544	544	544	544	544	544	6 163	
3 008	3 008	3 008	3 008	3 011	3 011	34 101	
399	399	399	399	399	399	4 519	
318	318	318	318	318	318	3 604	
223	223	223	223	223	223	2 523	
6 178	6 178	6 178	6 178	6 185	6 185	70 046	
318	318	318	318	318	318	3 604	
4 768	4 768	4 768	4 768	4 773	4 773	54 060	
4 768	4 768	4 768	4 768	4 773	4 773	54 060	
636	636	636	636	636	636	7 208	
24 158	24 158	24 158	24 158	24 186	24 186	273 904	
31 469	31 469	31 469	31 469	31 505	31 505	356 796	
954	954	954	954	955	955	10 812	
318	318	318	318	318	318	3 604	
126 562	*126 562*	*126 562*	*126 562*	*126 676*	*126 676*	*1 452 426*	
	-41 409		-41 409		-41 463	-232 598	
94 487	*53 077*	*94 487*	*53 077*	*94 624*	*53 160*	*821 197*	
7 147	7 231	7 315	7 401	7 487	7 574	85 342	
4 487	4 403	4 319	4 233	4 147	4 060	54 266	
82 853	*41 443*	*82 853*	*41 443*	*82 990*	*41 526*	*681 589*	
82 853	41 443	82 853	41 443	82 990	41 526	681 589	
23%	11%	23%	11%	23%	11%	17%	
25 210	25 210	25 210	25 210	25 210	25 210	302 525	
115 040						222 724	
565 093	**581 326**	**638 968**	**655 202**	**712 981**	**729 297**	**729 297**	

		NTOMBI'S MILK MARKET		CASHFLOW FORECAST		
Annual CPIX increase factor:	1.080	May-12	Jun-12	Jul-12	Aug-12	Sep-12
Percentage of total sales per month	1	0.0736	0.0736	0.0784	0.0784	0.0833
Sales	4 437 245	326 581	326 581	347 880	347 880	369 622
INCOME:						
Sales	4 437 245	326 581	326 581	347 880	347 880	369 622
Total Income:		**326 581**	**326 581**	**347 880**	**347 880**	**369 622**
COST OF SALES:						
Cost of sales	39%	127 367	127 367	135 673	135 673	144 153
Total Cost Sales		**127 367**	**127 367**	**135 673**	**135 673**	**144 153**
Gross profit		199 215	199 215	212 207	212 207	225 470
Gross profit %		61%	61%	61%	61%	61%
OPERATING EXPENDITURE						
Advertising and promotions	2.00%	6 532	6 532	6 958	6 958	7 392
Bank services charges	0.23%	751	751	800	800	850
Credit card charges	1.14%	3 723	3 723	3 966	3 966	4 214
Cleaning Materials	0.15%	490	490	522	522	554
First Aid	0.03%	98	98	104	104	111
Insurance	0.30%	980	980	1 044	1 044	1 109
Insurance Vehicles	0.00%	0	0	0	0	0
Laundry	0.06%	196	196	209	209	222
Licenses and Permits	0.11%	359	359	383	383	407
Medical Aid	0.00%	0	0	0	0	0
Motor expense						
Petrol	0.00%	2 000	2 000	2 000	2 000	2 000
Motor expense - other	0.00%	0	0	3 500	0	0
Postage and Delivery	0.01%	33	33	35	35	37
Printing and reproduction	0.05%	163	163	174	174	185
Professional fees						
Accounting	0.23%	751	751	800	800	850
Consulting	0.10%	327	327	348	348	370
Protective clothing	0.14%	457	457	487	487	517
Refreshments	0.00%	0	0	0	0	0
Refuse removal	0.10%	327	327	348	348	370
Rent (fixed)	29040	29 040	29 040	29 040	29 040	29 040
Repairs	0.00%					
Building repairs	0.09%	294	294	313	313	333
Computer repairs	0.03%	98	98	104	104	111
Equipment repairs	0.34%	1 110	1 110	1 183	1 183	1 257
Rates and Taxes	0.09%	294	294	313	313	333
Security	0.12%	392	392	417	417	444
Stationary and printing	0.11%	359	359	383	383	407
Subscriptions	0.02%	65	65	70	70	74
Telephone	0.00%	1 500	1 500	1 500	1 500	1 500
Fax	0.05%	163	163	174	174	185
Mobile	0.00%	0	0	0	0	0
Telephone - other	0.10%	327	327	348	348	370
Replacement of machinery	0.50%	1 633	1 633	1 739	1 739	1 848
Travel and entertainment						
Entertainment	0.00%	0	0	0	0	0
Travel	0.00%	0	0	0	0	0
Travel and entertainment - other	0.00%	0	0	0	0	0
Utilities	0.00%					
Water	0.15%	490	490	522	522	554
Gas and Electric	0.83%	2 711	2 711	2 887	2 887	3 068
Uniforms	0.11%	359	359	383	383	407
Unemployment insurance fund	0.09%	286	286	305	305	324
Workman's compensation fund	0.06%	201	201	214	214	227
Installment vehicle	1.71%	5 568	5 568	5 931	5 931	6 302
Gifts and donations	0.09%	286	286	305	305	324
Member Salary - A	1.32%	4 297	4 297	4 577	4 577	4 863
Member salary - B	1.32%	4 297	4 297	4 577	4 577	4 863
RSC Levy	0.18%	573	573	610	610	648
Salaries	6.67%	21 772	21 772	23 192	23 192	24 641
Wages	8.68%	28 361	28 361	30 211	30 211	32 099
Staff meals	0.26%	859	859	915	915	973
Skills Development	0.09%	286	286	305	305	324
Total operations expenditure (incl VAT):		*122 809*	*122 809*	*132 196*	*128 696*	*134 705*
VAT at 14%			-35 662		-38 047	
Total net profit (after accounting for VAT):		*76 406*	*40 744*	*80 011*	*45 464*	*90 764*
FINANCING EXPENSES						
Capital repayment		7 663	7 752	7 842	7 934	8 027
Interest		3 971	3 882	3 792	3 700	3 607
Total cash flow after financing repayments:		*64 772*	*29 110*	*68 377*	*33 830*	*79 130*
Retained cash per month	Nett Profit	64 772	29 110	68 377	33 830	79 130
	Nett Profit %	20%	9%	20%	10%	21%
Dividend payment		44 738	44 738	44 738	44 738	44 738
Tax payment		115 040				
Cashflow position		634 291	618 664	642 303	631 396	665 789
	R 729 296.57	Start fin year				

MAY 2012 TO APR 2013	Realistic scenario							
Oct-12	**Nov-12**	**Dec-12**	**Jan-13**	**Feb-13**	**Mar-13**	**Apr-13**	**TOTAL**	
0.0833	0.0882	0.0882	0.0882	0.0882	0.0883	0.0883	1	0
369 622	391 365	391 365	391 365	391 365	391 809	391 809	**4 437 245**	
369 622	391 365	391 365	391 365	391 365	391 809	391 809	4 437 245	
369 622	**391 365**	**391 365**	**391 365**	**391 365**	**391 809**	**391 809**	4 437 245	100.0%
								100%
144 153	152 632	152 632	152 632	152 632	152 805	152 805	1 730 525	
144 153	**152 632**	**152 632**	**152 632**	**152 632**	**152 805**	**152 805**	1 730 525	
225 470	238 733	238 733	238 733	238 733	239 003	239 003	**2 706 719**	
61%	61%	61%	61%	61%	61%	61%	61%	
7 392	7 827	7 827	7 827	7 827	7 836	7 836	88 745	
850	900	900	900	900	901	901	10 206	
4 214	4 462	4 462	4 462	4 462	4 467	4 467	50 585	
554	587	587	587	587	588	588	6 656	
111	117	117	117	117	118	118	1 331	
1 109	1 174	1 174	1 174	1 174	1 175	1 175	13 312	
0	0	0	0	0	0	0	0	
222	235	235	235	235	235	235	2 662	
407	431	431	431	431	431	431	4 881	
0	0	0	0	0	0	0	0	
							0	
2 000	2 000	2 000	2 000	2 000	2 000	2 000	24 000	
0	3 000	0	0	0	0	0	6 500	
37	39	39	39	39	39	39	444	
185	196	196	196	196	196	196	2 219	
850	900	900	900	900	901	901	10 206	
370	391	391	391	391	392	392	4 437	
517	548	548	548	548	549	549	6 212	
0	0	0	0	0	0	0	0	
370	391	391	391	391	392	392	4 437	
29 040	29 040	29 040	29 040	29 040	29 040	29 040	348 480	
							0	
333	352	352	352	352	353	353	3 994	
111	117	117	117	117	118	118	1 331	
1 257	1 331	1 331	1 331	1 331	1 332	1 332	15 087	
333	352	352	352	352	353	353	3 994	
444	470	470	470	470	470	470	5 325	
407	431	431	431	431	431	431	4 881	
74	78	78	78	78	78	78	887	
1 500	1 500	1 500	1 500	1 500	1 500	1 500	18 000	
185	196	196	196	196	196	196	2 219	
0	0	0	0	0	0	0	0	
370	391	391	391	391	392	392	4 437	
1 848	1 957	1 957	1 957	1 957	1 959	1 959	22 186	
							0	
0	0	0	0	0	0	0	0	
0	0	0	0	0	0	0	0	
0	0	0	0	0	0	0	0	
554	587	587	587	587	588	588	6 656	
3 068	3 248	3 248	3 248	3 248	3 252	3 252	36 829	
407	431	431	431	431	431	431	4 881	
324	343	343	343	343	344	344	3 892	
227	240	240	240	240	241	241	2 725	
6 302	6 672	6 672	6 672	6 672	6 680	6 680	75 649	
324	343	343	343	343	344	344	3 892	
4 863	5 150	5 150	5 150	5 150	5 155	5 155	58 385	
4 863	5 150	5 150	5 150	5 150	5 155	5 155	58 385	
648	687	687	687	687	687	687	7 785	
24 641	26 091	26 091	26 091	26 091	26 121	26 121	295 816	
32 099	33 987	33 987	33 987	33 987	34 025	34 025	385 340	
973	1 030	1 030	1 030	1 030	1 031	1 031	11 677	
324	343	343	343	343	344	344	3 892	
134 705	*143 715*	*140 715*	*140 715*	*140 715*	*140 838*	*140 838*	*1 623 456*	
-41 350		-43 855		-44 224		-44 282	-247 419	
49 414	95 017	54 162	98 017	53 794	98 165	53 883	835 844	
8 120	8 215	8 311	8 408	8 506	8 605	8 705	98 088	
3 514	3 419	3 323	3 226	3 128	3 029	2 929	41 520	
37 780	*83 383*	*42 528*	*86 383*	*42 160*	*86 531*	*42 249*	*696 236*	
37 780	83 383	42 528	86 383	42 160	86 531	42 249	696 236	
10%	21%	11%	22%	11%	22%	11%	16%	
44 738	44 738	44 738	44 738	44 738	44 738	44 738	536 852	
	121 517						236 557	
658 831	575 960	573 751	615 396	612 819	654 612	652 124	652 124	

143

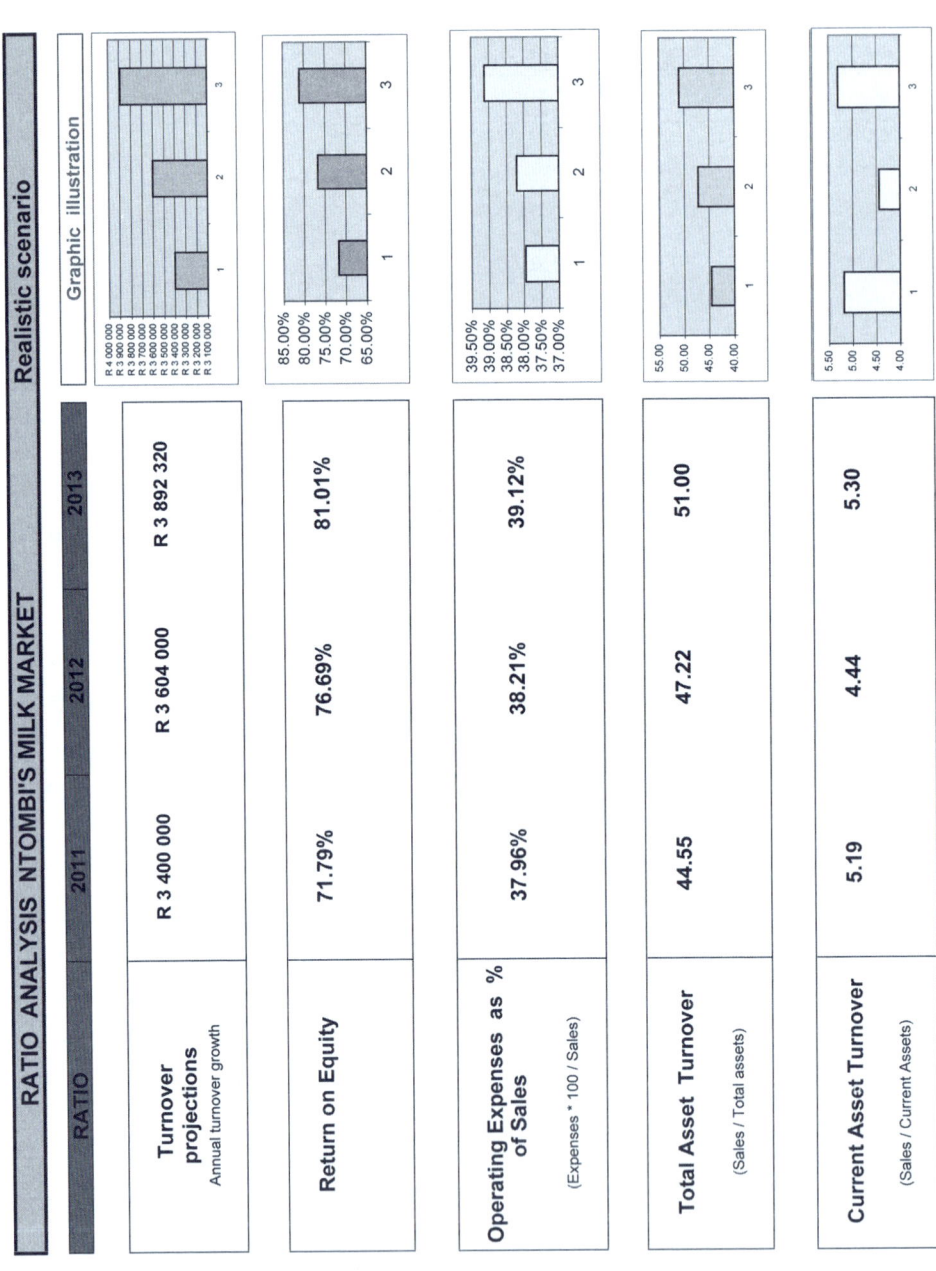

RATIO ANALYSIS NTOMBI'S MILK MARKET — Realistic scenario

RATIO	2011	2012	2013	Graphic illustration
Turnover projections Annual turnover growth	R 3 400 000	R 3 604 000	R 3 892 320	
Return on Equity	71.79%	76.69%	81.01%	
Operating Expenses as % of Sales (Expenses * 100 / Sales)	37.96%	38.21%	39.12%	
Total Asset Turnover (Sales / Total assets)	44.55	47.22	51.00	
Current Asset Turnover (Sales / Current Assets)	5.19	4.44	5.30	

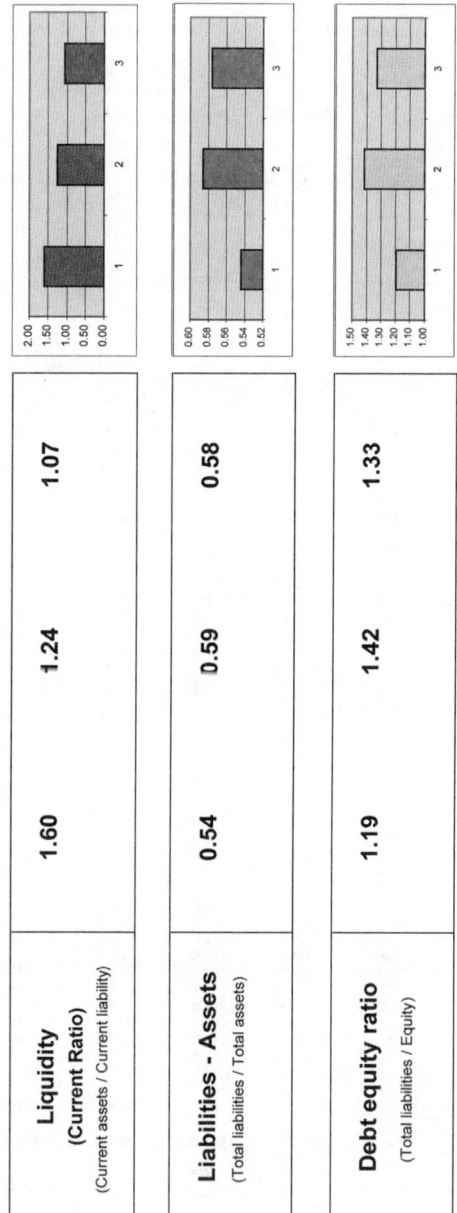

| **Liquidity** **(Current Ratio)** (Current assets / Current liability) | 1.60 | 1.24 | 1.07 |

| **Liabilities - Assets** (Total liabilities / Total assets) | 0.54 | 0.59 | 0.58 |

| **Debt equity ratio** (Total liabilities / Equity) | 1.19 | 1.42 | 1.33 |

	May-12	Jun-12	Jul-12	Aug-12	Sep-12	Oct-12	Nov-12
			NTOMBI'S MILK MARKET			**Break even forecast :**	
Sales	285 274	285 274	303 878	303 878	322 871	322 871	341 863
Fixed Costs							
Cost of sales	111 257	111 257	118 513	118 513	125 920	125 920	133 327
G & A (w/o Depreciation)							
Depreciation							
Less Reclassified Fixed Costs							
Total Fixed Costs	**111 257**	**111 257**	**118 513**	**118 513**	**125 920**	**125 920**	**133 327**
Variable Costs							
Advertising and promotions	5 705	5 705	6 078	6 078	6 457	6 457	6 837
Bank services charges	656	656	699	699	743	743	786
Credit card charges	3 252	3 252	3 464	3 464	3 681	3 681	3 897
Cleaning Materials	428	428	456	456	484	484	513
First Aid	86	86	91	91	97	97	103
Insurance	856	856	912	912	969	969	1 026
Insurance Vehicles	0	0	0	0	0	0	0
Laundry	171	171	182	182	194	194	205
Licenses and Permits	314	314	334	334	355	355	376
Medical Aid	0	0	0	0	0	0	0
Motor expense							
Petrol	1 000	0	0	0	0	0	0
Motor expense - other	0	0	0	0	0	0	0
Postage and Delivery	29	29	30	30	32	32	34
Printing and reproduction	143	143	152	152	161	161	171
Professional fees							
Accounting	656	656	699	699	743	743	786
Consulting	285	285	304	304	323	323	342
Protective clothing	399	399	425	425	452	452	479
Refreshments	0	0	0	0	0	0	0
Refuse removal	285	285	304	304	323	323	342
Rent (fixed)	24 000	24 000	24 000	24 000	24 000	24 000	24 000
Repairs							
Building repairs	257	257	273	273	291	291	308
Computer repairs	86	86	91	91	97	97	103
Equipment repairs	970	970	1 033	1 033	1 098	1 098	1 162
Rates and Taxes	257	257	273	273	291	291	308
Security	342	342	365	365	387	387	410
Stationary and printing	314	314	334	334	355	355	376
Subscriptions	57	57	61	61	65	65	68
Telephone							
Fax	143	143	152	152	161	161	171
Mobile	0	0	0	0	0	0	0
Telephone - other	285	285	304	304	323	323	342
Replacement of machinery	1 426	1 426	1 519	1 519	1 614	1 614	1 709
Travel and entertainment							
Entertainment	0	0	0	0	0	0	0
Travel	0	0	0	0	0	0	0
Travel and entertainment - other	0	0	0	0	0	0	0
Utilities							
Water	428	428	456	456	484	484	513
Gas and Electric	2 368	2 368	2 522	2 522	2 680	2 680	2 837
Uniforms	314	314	334	334	355	355	376
Unemployment insurance fund	250	250	267	267	283	283	300
Workman's compensation fund	175	175	187	187	198	198	210
Installment vehicle	4 864	4 864	5 181	5 181	5 505	5 505	5 828
Gifts and donations	250	250	267	267	283	283	300
Member Salary - A	3 754	3 754	3 998	3 998	4 248	4 248	4 498
Member salary - B	3 754	3 754	3 998	3 998	4 248	4 248	4 498
RSC Levy	500	500	533	533	566	566	600
Salaries	19 018	19 018	20 259	20 259	21 525	21 525	22 791
Wages	24 774	24 774	26 389	26 389	28 039	28 039	29 688
Staff meals	751	751	800	800	850	850	900
Skills Development	250	250	267	267	283	283	300
Total Variable Costs	**103 851**	**102 851**	**107 993**	**107 993**	**113 243**	**113 243**	**118 493**
Income from Operations	**70 166**	**71 166**	**77 372**	**77 372**	**83 708**	**83 708**	**90 044**
Capital repayment	-5 801	-5 868	-5 937	-6 006	-6 076	-6 147	-6 219
Interest	-5 833	-5 766	-5 697	-5 628	-5 558	-5 487	-5 415
Income Taxes - "Variable"	0	-31 808	0	-34 267	0	-36 777	0
Net Income After Taxes	**58 532**	**27 723**	**65 738**	**31 471**	**72 074**	**35 297**	**78 410**
Income from Operations Analysis							
Contribution Margin	63.60%	63.95%	64.46%	64.46%	64.93%	64.93%	65.34%
Break-Even Sales Volume	174 943	173 984	183 850	183 850	193 943	193 943	204 053
Sales Volume Above Break-Even	110 331	111 290	120 028	120 028	128 928	128 928	137 810
Net Income After Taxes Analysis							
Contribution Margin	63.60%	52.80%	64.46%	53.18%	64.93%	53.54%	65.34%
Break-Even Sales Volume	174 943	270 975	183 850	287 261	193 943	303 905	204 053
Sales Volume Above Break-Even	110 331	14 299	120 028	16 617	128 928	18 966	137 810

MAY 2012 TO APR 2013				Realistic scenario		
Dec-12	**Jan-13**	**Feb-13**	**Mar-13**	**Apr-13**	**TOTAL**	**% of Total Sales**
341 863	341 863	341 863	342 251	342 251	**3 876 000**	
133 327	133 327	133 327	133 478	133 478	**1 511 640**	39.00%
					0	0.00%
					0	0.00%
					0	0.00%
133 327	**133 327**	**133 327**	**133 478**	**133 478**	**1 511 640**	39.00%
6 837	6 837	6 837	6 845	6 845	**77 520**	2.00%
786	786	786	787	787	**8 915**	0.23%
3 897	3 897	3 897	3 902	3 902	**44 186**	1.14%
513	513	513	513	513	**5 814**	0.15%
103	103	103	103	103	**1 163**	0.03%
1 026	1 026	1 026	1 027	1 027	**11 628**	0.30%
0	0	0	0	0	**0**	0.00%
205	205	205	205	205	**2 326**	0.06%
376	376	376	376	376	**4 264**	0.11%
0	0	0	0	0	**0**	0.00%
					0	0.00%
0	0	0	0	0	**1 000**	0.03%
0	0	0	0	0	**0**	0.00%
34	34	34	34	34	**388**	0.01%
171	171	171	171	171	**1 938**	0.05%
					0	0.00%
786	786	786	787	787	**8 915**	0.23%
342	342	342	342	342	**3 876**	0.10%
479	479	479	479	479	**5 426**	0.14%
0	0	0	0	0	**0**	0.00%
342	342	342	342	342	**3 876**	0.10%
24 000	24 000	24 000	24 000	24 000	**288 000**	7.43%
					0	
308	308	308	308	308	**3 488**	0.09%
103	103	103	103	103	**1 163**	0.03%
1 162	1 162	1 162	1 164	1 164	**13 178**	0.34%
308	308	308	308	308	**3 488**	0.09%
410	410	410	411	411	**4 651**	0.12%
376	376	376	376	376	**4 264**	0.11%
68	68	68	68	68	**775**	0.02%
					0	
171	171	171	171	171	**1 938**	0.05%
0	0	0	0	0	**0**	0.00%
342	342	342	342	342	**3 876**	0.10%
1 709	1 709	1 709	1 711	1 711	**19 380**	0.50%
					0	
0	0	0	0	0	**0**	0.00%
0	0	0	0	0	**0**	0.00%
0	0	0	0	0	**0**	0.00%
					0	
513	513	513	513	513	**5 814**	0.15%
2 837	2 837	2 837	2 841	2 841	**32 171**	0.83%
376	376	376	376	376	**4 264**	0.11%
300	300	300	300	300	**3 400**	0.09%
210	210	210	210	210	**2 380**	0.06%
5 828	5 828	5 828	5 835	5 835	**66 081**	1.70%
300	300	300	300	300	**3 400**	0.09%
4 498	4 498	4 498	4 503	4 503	**51 000**	1.32%
4 498	4 498	4 498	4 503	4 503	**51 000**	1.32%
600	600	600	600	600	**6 800**	0.18%
22 791	22 791	22 791	22 817	22 817	**258 400**	6.67%
29 688	29 688	29 688	29 722	29 722	**336 600**	8.68%
900	900	900	901	901	**10 200**	0.26%
300	300	300	300	300	**3 400**	0.09%
118 493	118 493	118 493	118 600	118 600	**1 360 345**	0.35
90 044	90 044	90 044	90 173	90 173	**1 004 015**	0.26
-6 291	-6 365	-6 439	-6 514	-6 590	**-74 253**	-1.92%
-5 343	-5 269	-5 195	-5 120	-5 044	**-65 355**	
-39 288	0	-39 288	0	-39 339	**-220 767**	-5.70%
39 122	78 410	39 122	78 539	39 200	**643 640**	16.61%
65.34%	65.34%	65.34%	65.35%	65.35%	**64.90%**	
204 053	204 053	204 053	204 260	204 260	**2 329 062**	60.09%
137 810	137 810	137 810	137 991	137 991	**1 546 938**	39.91%
53.85%	65.34%	53.85%	65.35%	53.85%	**74.20%**	
320 564	204 053	320 564	204 260	320 905	**2 334 750**	60.24%
21 299	137 810	21 299	137 991	21 346	**1 541 250**	39.76%

7. Critical risks

The following table shows the potential risks identified in the business environment applicable to Ntombi's Milk Market, as well as the way it will be managed accordingly:

Potential risks:	Mitigation:
Lower supply of milk	Backward integration (acquisition of diary farm)
Increased transport costs	Increase capacity for higher volume production
Labour strikes	Market-related salaries/wages, clean and satisfying work environment, continuous motivation
Negative hygienic conditions	Appointment of more cleaners and effective cleaning material
Increased competition	Higher levels of product differentiation

Comprehensive directory of national small-business services

Absa: The bank presently hands out the most Khula bank guarantees to small businesses and is probably your best chance of getting a bank loan approved. (011) 350 4000. www.absa.co.za.

Black Business Supplier Development Programme (BBSDP): Helps black-owned businesses to become more competitive. 0861 843 384.

Black Management Forum: Business training and networking. (011) 784 4407.

Business Beat: Assists small business owners with advice, mentoring, bookkeeping and company registration. (021) 448 9075.

Business Partners: Provides equity and bridging finance as well as mentoring for viable businesses. (011) 470 8700. www.businesspartners.co.za.

Companies and Intellectual Property Registration Office (CIPRO): To register your company, trademark or patent you need to contact CIPRO. 0861 843 384. www.cipro.co.za.

Council for Scientific and Industrial Research (CSIR): Assists business owners who want to improve on or develop a product with market-related research and product testing. (012) 841 2911. www.csir.co.za.

DTI's customer contact number: For general DTI queries, assistance and information contact 0861 843 384. www.dti.gov.za.

Dutch Program for Cooperation with Emerging Markets (PSOM) was officially launched in South Africa last year to assist small business owners with Dutch–South African partnership opportunities. It covers half of all the linkage costs. (012) 939 9447.

Enterprise Competition: This is an annual national competition. The people behind the selected business ideas receive intensive business training. (011) 482 9697.

Export Market Investment Assistance (EMIA): Provides funding to small business exporters and focuses on assisting business owners with trade missions and attending exhibitions, but also provides funding for things such as marketing, patent registration and export-readiness training. 0861 843 384.

Franchise Advice and Information Network (FRAIN): This is a web-based information and support service connected with aspects of franchising such as what franchises are available, how to franchise, as well as the financial and legal implications attached to franchising. (012) 349 0100. www.frain.co.za.

Franchising Association of South Africa (FASA): requires member franchises to subscribe to a set of rules. It is usually a good sign if the franchise you want to buy belongs to FASA. (011) 484 1285. www.fasa.co.za.

Industrial Development Corporation (IDC): Business owners who have a turnover of at least R1 million and who have secured contracts but require large amounts of short-term capital to fund a project can request the IDC's bridging finance. The construction sector is excluded from this type of funding. (011) 269 3000. www.idc.co.za.

Khethani Business Finance: This is a non-profit organisation that assists with finance for small businesses whose loan applications would normally be turned down by the banks. (011) 781 7224.

Khula Enterprise: Business owners who have difficulty finding bank loans because of a lack of collateral can approach the DTI's small business finance organisation for Khula-guaranteed bank loans. These include, amongst others, the Individual Guarantee Scheme for loans of R1 million or less; and the Emerging Entrepreneur Scheme for loans of less than R2 million. (012) 394 5560. www.khula.org.za.

National African Federated Chamber of Commerce (NAFCOC): Represents the interests of black business and provides networking and lobbying for small business members. (011) 268 2800. www.nafcoc.org.za.

National Empowerment Fund (NEF): This fund provides acquisition funding and venture capital in support of black empowerment from R200 000 upwards. (011) 772 8000. www.nefcorp.co.za.

National Productivity Institute (NPI): A non-governmental organisation which has various subsidised programmes and solutions for small business owners wanting to increase their productivity. (012) 341 1470.

Netherlands Management Cooperation Program (NMCP): A Dutch support programme for local businesses. The programme offers to fly retired business consultants to South Africa, at the programme's expense, to assist the business with loans, equipment and development funds. The business in South Africa would be responsible for the consultant's accommodation expenses. (021) 951 6852.

Nexus Financial Solutions: This is a Sanlam one-stop business website and call centre for businesses which have been in operation for longer than two years. The site refers owners to various services ranging from legal issues to tax and financial assistance. 0860 100 539. www.npi.co.za.

Old Mutual small retailer consulting services: Old Mutual Properties have introduced a support service to small retailers who are tenants in any of their shopping malls. This service helps to train and mentor the retailer so that they become more competitive. (021) 424 5280.

Progress Fund: The fund provides loans and equity finance to businesses owned by young, previously disadvantaged people between the ages of 18 and 35 years. (011) 371 6679. www.fnb.co.za.

Proudly South African: This is a branding campaign to promote South African products by carrying the Proudly South African logo. Business owners can place the logo on their products at a cost of 0.1% of the sales of their product. (011) 327 7778. www.proudlysa.co.za.

Sector Partnership Fund: Assists groups of small business owners and micro entrepreneurs in the manufacturing, IT and agro-processing sectors with grants to link up and pool resources in order to meet a tender which otherwise may be too big for them to do alone. 0861 843 384. www.dti.gov.za.

Sizanani: Arranges guarantees for small businesses with little or no collateral, while providing mentoring services to go hand-in-hand with the bank guarantees. 0861 333 000.

Small Business Project: Assists small businesses through their Linkage Programme with link-ups and joint ventures with corporates. (011) 484 4666. www.sbp.org.za.

Small and Medium Enterprise Development Programme (SMEDP): Provides grants to small businesses in manufacturing, tourism, agro-processing, IT, arts and crafts, aqua culture and high-value agricultures which require training or land, machinery or buildings for expanding existing projects or starting up new ones. 0861 843 384.

Small Enterprise Development Agency (SEDA): The government's agency for business support. SEDA funds the Manufacturing Advice Centres (MAC) programme where manufacturers and businesses in select business sectors can get up to 90% of their business support intervention sponsored. It also funds local business support centres and tender advice centres. 0860 103 703. www.seda.org.za.

SMME Africa: This is an annual Africa-wide competition which honours top African business-owner nominees in various categories. It was held for the first time in 2003 and is organised by the Centre for Investment Analysis at the University of Stellenbosch. (021) 918 4258.

Softstart: A Gauteng-based technology hub which is situated inside the CSIR campus. The incubator also assists technical businesses outside the province and offers mentoring, product-development, finance referral and business plan assistance. (012) 349 2355. www.softstart.co.za.

South African Breweries (SAB) Kickstart: An annual national competition organised and sponsored by SAB-Miller, which has been running for eight years now. Business owners and entrepreneurs who enter the competition are also enrolled in a Kickstart training programme. (021) 658 7395.

South African Bureau of Standards (SABS): Assists small businesses with accreditation of products and services with a 50% subsidy. (012) 428 6110. www.sabs.co.za.

South African Chamber of Business (SACOB): Assists with networking, website services, lobbying and business information. (011) 446 3800. www.sacob.co.za.

South Africa International Business Linkages (SAIBL): A US government-sponsored fund which aims to assist historically disadvantaged South African small businesses to grow through funding, as well as linking them up with trade and investment partnerships, both in South Africa and internationally. (011) 802 0015.

South African Revenue Service (SARS): (011) 374 8000. www.sars.gov.za.

Standard Bank: The leader in small-business development for many years, with a huge range of products and services for the business owner. (011) 636 9112. www.standardbank.co.za.

Support Programme for Industrial Innovation (SPII): Provides innovation support and offers grants to small businesses for new product and process development. SPII is funded by the DTI and administered by the IDC. (011) 269 3000.

Swedish–South African Business Fund: A Swedish fund which aims to support historically disadvantaged South African small businesses and provide them with linkages and joint ventures with Swedish firms. The fund contributes 50% of external costs, such as travel and setting up an alliance. (011) 784 8087.

Technology and Human Resources for Industry Programme (THRIP): Managed under the National Research Foundation (NRF), THRIP provides incentive funding for research and technological advancement to business owners. (012) 481 4078.

Technology for Women in Business (TWIB): Provides various technology-advice programmes and training opportunities aimed specifically at women who want to expand and enhance their business through the use of computers, science and the latest equipment. (012) 841 4983. www.twib.co.za.

Tender Advice Centres (TACs): Assists business owners with securing government tenders and is also a good place to access business training and financial assistance. Most of their services are free or highly subsidised. 0860 103 703. www.seda.org.za.

Tradeworld: Provides tender information and business opportunities daily via fax or email (011) 507 0900. www.tradeworld.net.

National Youth Development Fund (NYDA): A fund aimed at young people between the ages of 18 and 35 operating in the franchising industry. (011) 480 8700. www.nyda.org.za.

Upstarts: Mark Shuttleworth started this technology incubator, which provides funding and assistance to small businesses across the country. Though based in Cape Town, it can act as a 'virtual hub' to businesses across the country. (021) 970 1500. www.upstarts.co.za.

Zimele Trust: Zimele provides funding through loan and equity finance to junior mining companies. (011) 638 3001. www.zimele.co.za.

Index

Page numbers in *italics* refer to figures and tables.

L

M

N

O

objectives of businesses 25, 66-68
   definition of 68
Occupational Health and Safety Act 107
operational function (operations management) 25, 113, 121
Outsurance 6

P

partnerships 64, 99, *100-102*, 111
Passion on a Plate 4
patents 52-53, 105
perseverance 9
personal characteristics of entrepreneurs 9-11
personal relations *see* human relations
personnel management *see* human resource function
physical environment 33-34
planning 13, 39-40, *39*, 60-61, *60*
   checklist 66
political environment 34-35
pollution 34
population, demographics of 31-32
positioning *see* market positioning
positive attitude 11
potential income *see* income
potential market 68-70, *69*
primary sector 22
private companies 65, 99, *100-102*
production branches 22, *22*
production factors of businesses 26
profit *see* expected net profit
pro forma income statements 77, *77-78*
psychographic segmentation 69-70
public companies 65, 99
public relations function 26, 113, 116-117
purchasing function 25, 113, 120-121

Q

quality, importance of 15

R

Receiver of Revenue 105-106 *see also* taxation
record systems function *see* information and record systems function
Registrar of Companies 103, 105, 111-112
relationships *see* human relations
re-sale market 28